Self-Hypnosis: Easy as 1, 2, 3

3 Minutes to Change Your Life!

D1611078

Joann Abrahamsen

www.joannabrahamsen.com

Self-Hypnosis: Easy as 1, 2, 3
3 Minutes to Change Your Life!

By Joann Abrahamsen

First Printing: July 2022

ISBN: 979-8-9866531-0-5

Permission granted to reprint the 3-step self-hypnosis procedure outlined in the NGH Certification Training with credit to Dr. Richard Harte and the National Guild of Hypnotists: www.NGH.net

Published by:
Change Your Life Press
9 The Crossway
Yonkers, NY 10701
(914) 476-8131
www.joannabrahamsen.com

Joann Abrahamsen is available to speak at your business or conference event on a variety of topics. Go to her website www.joannabrahamsen.com and send her an email.

Joann Abrahamsen

Hypnosis For a Change

9 The Crossway

Yonkers, NY 10701

914-476-8131

www.joannabrahamsen.com

This book is the first in a series of self-help books. Future books in this self-help series will discuss weight loss, cancer issues, stop smoking, memory and learning, and others.

Go to my website www.joannabrahamsen.com and click on the offer *Reprogram Your Subconscious Mind*. You will then be on my mailing list, and you will be notified of future books.

As a special bonus to the first twenty-five people who email me after reading this book, *Self-Hypnosis: Easy as 1, 2, 3*, you can go to my website and send me an email, and I will help you formulate your suggestions. This offer is only open to the first twenty-five people who send me an email. Put "Formulate a self-hypnosis suggestion" in the subject line. Tell me what your goal is and include the suggestion you formulated. I will reply via email. If you provide me with a phone number, I may call you.

If you would like to discuss your goals with me and book an online session, click on the link for a free Zoom consultation. Download the free *Reprogram Your Subconscious Mind* while you are there.

Joann Abrahamsen is available to speak at your business or conference event on a variety of topics. Go to her website www.joannabrahamsen.com and send her an email.

What Others Are Saying

"This book is unique, and the self-hypnosis method Joann offers is amazing! You will formulate your own powerful suggestions based on the habit(s) you want to change and apply them in just three minutes. It's like speed-trance for self-hypnosis! Her book includes suggestions for weight management, stopping smoking, peak performance, sales, memory and learning, and many other applications. Joann's book delivers on the promise that in just three minutes a day, you can change just about anything."

—Dr. Richard Nongard,
author of *The Self-Hypnosis Solution*

"Learning self-hypnosis has many benefits. After suffering a permanent back injury in the early 1980s, I discovered the benefits of hypnosis and self-hypnosis for taming chronic pain enough to live a normal life...and decided to become a hypnotherapist. I met Joann Abrahamsen in 1989 at a national hypnosis convention in New York City and learned firsthand how skilled she is. Although I had already been hypnotized many times, I am analytical and could count on one hand the number of times I was ever able to attain a deep level of hypnosis. Joann was able to get me deeper than anyone, including the legendary Charles Tebbetts, who was my original hypnosis instructor. Read her book...she has mastered the art of hypnosis."

—Roy Hunter, hypnosis trainer and author *of The Art of Hypnosis* and coauthor of *The Art of Hypnotic Regression Therapy*

"Joann Abrahamsen has created one of the easiest self-hypnosis books I have ever read. Her sub-title says it all: 3 Minutes to Change Your Life! Without spending too much time, you learn the self-hypnosis skills quickly and apply them easily. Joann relates to her readers with her easy style and clear writing. She discusses and demystifies hypnosis and talks a little bit about how she became involved with hypnosis. I plan on recommending this book to my students and clients. Read this book to learn how easy it can be to change your life and become the person you want to be in three easy steps."

—Larry Garrett, certified consulting hypnotist and author of *Healing the Enemy* and *Hypnotizing the Devil*

"Joann Abrahamsen's book certainly makes self-hypnosis as easy as 1-2-3. You can change your life in just three minutes when you learn her techniques. She writes in the same style as she teaches: uncomplicated, right to the point, and brimming with real information and guidance. As a certified consulting hypnotist for over fifty years, I see this work as more than a self-help aid. Joann's book is a boon to teachers instructing in self-hypnosis, an aid to therapists helping others to make change, as well as those who want to learn the proven Abrahamsen techniques to take charge of their lives. Her book is a welcome gift to our society much in need of a guiding light for achievement and success."

—Maurice Kershaw MA., president & executive director of Canadian Institute of Hypnotism

"Joann is a master hypnotist and teacher. She has added writing to her amazing skill level. This book is practical, easy to understand, and ready to use for self-improvement. 'Every day in every way, I get better and better' will lead you into positive change."

—Marty Lerman PhD, certified hypnotherapist and author of *Mindshift: Your Life Doesn't Have to Suck*

"Your self-hypnosis instructions are very effective, especially how you explain how to formulate suggestions. I was impressed with your techniques."

"Folks, Joann and I have been associates for twenty-five plus years now, and she knows so much about hypnosis. She is a great educator, and I think you will find her instructions easy to follow and learn. She covers it all regarding self-hypnosis, and you will find it easy to be hypnotizing yourself soon! This book is a jewel that novices and veterans alike should have in their libraries. Learn self-hypnosis and change your life!"

"Most people use self-hypnosis but do not realize they are using it. For example, a lot of people entertain negative thoughts like, 'I can't do that,' or 'It's not going to work.' Some people use positive thoughts like, 'I can do that,' or 'I will make that work.' The secret is to maintain positive thoughts. Read Joann's book and learn how to create positive suggestions. Her book is very enlightening and shows you how to accomplish your goals. Joann will teach you how to tap into the power of your mind to accomplish any goal you want."

TABLE OF CONTENTS

ABOUT THE AUTHOR

J oann Abrahamsen is a National Guild of Hypnotists board-certified consultant in hypnosis and was inducted into the NGH's Order of Braid, recognizing a lifetime of outstanding achievement, dedication, and service. Joann also received the NGH Outstanding Achievement Award.

Currently, she writes a quarterly column for the *Journal of Hypnotism* and was featured on the cover of the March 2022 issue. Abrahamsen was named the Association to Advance Ethical Hypnosis' 1992 "Person of the Year" and was the recipient of both the President's Award and the Harry Arons Award.

She is certified in neuro-linguistic programming and life coaching by the International Certification Board of Clinical Hypnotherapists (ICBCH). Joann was inducted into the Hypnosis Hall of Fame in 1990 and named "Best of Yonkers" for hypnosis services for three years in a row.

Currently, she is writing another soon-to-be-published book, A Potpourri of Hypnotic Techniques. Future books will include Surviving and Thriving after a Cancer Diagnosis; Weight Management: Help with Hypnosis; Stop Smoking, and others.

When she is not writing, Joann, along with her husband, Robert Fried, enjoys ballroom dancing and traveling, especially cruising. Joann and Robert live in Westchester County, NY with their fancy calico cat, Nutmeg.

Foreword

by C. Roy Hunter, DIMDHA, DAPHP

"Much, perhaps too much, has been written about hypnosis: what it is or is not; whether it is or is not possible to hypnotize another person, or become hypnotized yourself; whether it is good or evil; or whether it even exists."

A medical professional wrote the above words in the Foreword of my hypnosis text published many years ago, so I added one more book to the numerous books written about hypnosis—and followed up with several more that are recommended in numerous hypnosis schools around the world.

Is it mind control? … NO! I know from personal experience how easy it is to reject a suggestion if I am not emotionally comfortable with it. Years ago, a psychotherapist hypnotized me deeply and then told me to shave off my beard. My reaction was to bring myself up out of hypnosis and give her a lecture on ethics. History provides numerous definitions of hypnosis, and even now, the debate continues among professionals.

Joann's book, however, is about self-hypnosis, which is very personal to me….

After suffering a permanent back injury in the early 1980s, I discovered the benefits of hypnosis and self-hypnosis for taming chronic pain enough to live a normal life; and in 1983, I decided to become a hypnotherapist. I studied at the Charles Tebbetts Hypnotism Training Institute. My instructor was a twentieth-century legend in our profession, although I did not realize that when I first enrolled in his course. Several months later, I received my certification.

As a hypnosis practitioner, I have literally taught self-hypnosis to tens of thousands of people over the years—both in private sessions and in group workshops. Learning self-hypnosis has many additional benefits. For example, self-hypnosis (often associated with mindfulness) has helped me manage stress over the years. During my years of teaching professional hypnosis and facilitating workshops, numerous medical professionals attending my classes and workshops almost unanimously warn about the impact of stress on the body and our health.

Furthermore, self-hypnosis and mindfulness enhance a person's ability to overcome undesired habits and achieve goals. I believe this skill is so valuable that I offer to teach it to almost all my clients.

Imagination is the language of the subconscious—and both hypnosis and self-hypnosis make it easier to imagine your desired outcomes. Additionally, imagining the benefits of achieving your goals and desires increases your emotional desire to do what it takes to manifest those goals because emotion is the motivating power of the mind.

The author of this book is a skilled hypnosis professional and trainer with many years of experience under her belt. I first met Joann Abrahamsen in 1989 at a national hypnosis convention in New York City and learned first-hand how skilled she is. Although I had already been hypnotized many times, I am analytical and could count on one hand the number of times I was able to attain a deep level of hypnosis since my certification. Joann was able to get me deeper than anyone, including the legendary Charles Tebbetts, my original hypnosis instructor.

In addition to working with many thousands of clients, Joann's experience includes facilitating workshops for other hypnosis professionals. She is well qualified to write books and share what works for her clients. Read her book…she has mastered the art of hypnosis.

—Roy Hunter, published author and hypnosis trainer

INTRODUCTION

There are many self-hypnosis books out there. This method of self-hypnosis is unique in that you give yourself the suggestion BEFORE you put yourself in hypnosis and allow the suggestion to go into your subconscious mind. With some other methods, you put yourself in hypnosis and then give yourself the suggestion. Because you are using your conscious mind when you give yourself suggestions, you are lightening the hypnotic state.

With this method of self-hypnosis, you give yourself the suggestion before you put yourself into hypnosis; therefore, the conscious critical mind is not active while you are in hypnosis, and the suggestion goes directly into the subconscious mind. I did not "invent" this method of self-hypnosis. The original idea of giving yourself a suggestion before you go into hypnosis originated with Harry Arons in his book, *Master Course in Hypnotism*. I knew Harry well, and he gave me his blessing to use this method of self-hypnosis. I've adopted his method and added my own touches. I teach this method of self-hypnosis to all my clients and to students I train for certification.

See my website and send me an email for more information about hypnosis training or to book a session with me for online hypnosis.

Website: www.joannabrahamsen.com

CHAPTER 1

Just 3 Minutes a Day

D
o you have three minutes a day to change your life? Within the pages of this book, you will learn a simple three-step method of self-hypnosis. Once you learn and practice the three steps, you can make profound changes in your life.

You can change anything you want. There are many self-help books on the market. They are all good at any one time in your life. However, most self-help books tell you that you need to change and what to change, but they do not tell you how to change. This book will not only tell you how, but it will explain how, step by step. You selected this book because this is the kind of book you need now! The answers lie within you.

In just three weeks, you will learn and practice a simple three-step self-hypnosis technique that will teach you how to put yourself into hypnosis, stay in hypnosis for three minutes, and then bring yourself out of hypnosis. When you finish this book, you will have the tools to construct suggestions for yourself to achieve any goal you desire. The self-hypnosis suggestion process only takes three minutes!

In the chapters that follow, we discuss many different areas where you can make improvements, such as: stopping smoking, managing weight, managing stress, increasing sales, overcoming bad habits, enhancing performance, memory and learning, self-esteem and motivation, and medical applications. If a chapter does not apply to you, then just skip it.

Change can be defined as: to make different, alter, pass from one condition or state to another. The key to making a change is that you must *want the results of the change more than doing the work and exerting the effort to obtain the results that you want.*

The method you will use to change your life and achieve your goals is called self-hypnosis. While hypnosis is used as the vehicle for the journey, you are the driver. You are in control of the car. This book is about you.

You are a wonderful person. Look at yourself in a mirror. Go ahead. I will wait.

Did you look? Good! What did you see? Yourself, of course. Many people look outside of themselves for the answer. Some turn to overeating, smoking, alcohol, drugs, or other people for the answers. But you are the answer. If you want to make a change and are ready to make the changes and do the work necessary to achieve your goals, then let us journey together.

Are you ready?

Hypnosis is not magic, but it is magical.

CHAPTER 2

How to Use This Book

You can read the entire book through if you like before you decide on an issue you want to work with, or you can turn to the chapter that addresses the issue you want to work with first.

If you want to work with a particular issue, I suggest you read until you get to Step 1. Start practicing Step 1 as you continue to read. Do not start practicing Step 2 until you have practiced Step 1 for a week. After a week, practice Step 2 as you continue to read. A week after you practice Step 2, you are ready to formulate your suggestions.

Before you formulate your suggestions, read the chapter that pertains to your issue. For example, you want to lose weight. Read Chapter 9 for examples on formulating suggestions for weight loss.

Review the chapter on how to formulate suggestions. After you formulate your suggestion meeting all the criteria, practice Step 3. You no longer do Steps 1 or 2. You can use a plain sheet of paper to copy the worksheet in this book. It's fine to continue to read the book while you're practicing Steps 1 and 2, but you should allow for a week's practice for Step 1 and let a second week pass as you practice Step 2. Beginning the third week, you formulate your suggestion and practice self-hypnosis. See additional instructions with each step.

Self-hypnosis works best if you give yourself the suggestion twice a day. However, if you only have time for one three-minute session, that's fine too.

You only need to read Chapters 1–7 to learn self-hypnosis and how to formulate suggestions. Then you can turn to the chapter(s) that address the issue(s) where you want to make a change. Just remember, while you may wish to focus on several issues, you should only tackle one issue at a time. You may need to change two different habits. For example, pertaining to weight management, you may eat too fast and eat larger portions. If you want to work on both at the same time, you can but do not combine them. Give yourself one suggestion in the morning to slow down your eating and the other suggestion to eat smaller portions in the afternoon. However, if you do this, it may take longer for each suggestion to "take hold." It can take up to three weeks for your suggestion(s) to become a habit. When the new suggestion becomes a habit, you can then formulate another suggestion.

You should only work on one issue at a time. You may want to lose weight and stop smoking, but you should choose the most important one first. When you are successful with that, then go on to the other issue.

As you go through the chapters, you will find some self-hypnosis suggestions repeated. You may turn to different chapters at different times and discover the same suggestion can apply to more than one situation.

We all collect books that address different changes we want to make in our lives. My own bookshelves are lined with self-help books regarding issues such as weight loss, stopping smoking, stress management, becoming more organized, improving your memory, overcoming procrastination, organizing your home, and many others. Most of these books were bought to give me ideas to help clients. You may need to refer to another book(s) for suggestions. For example, if you need to learn how to cook healthier, you may have to get a book that teaches you how to reduce the fat in your cooking or how to make healthier food choices. If you want to improve your sales performance, you may want to refer to a book on sales. If you want to play a better game of golf, you may have to seek help from a golf pro who will help you improve your game, and then you could formulate your suggestion(s) around acquiring the correct habit(s) you need to play better golf.

In some chapters, I give you a technique to use for a specific issue. For example, in the chapter "Medical Applications," I explain the control room technique for reducing the pain level. You put yourself into hypnosis and practice the technique. Your self-hypnosis suggestion can then be worded: "As I practice the control room technique, I dial down the discomfort, and I feel great." Then, for the three minutes you are in hypnosis, you imagine yourself being in a control room, reducing the discomfort level. In the memory and learning chapter, I explain the rehearsal technique. In the stress management chapter, I explain the 3, 2, 1 technique. In another chapter, I explain the reframing technique. You can mix and match any technique to obtain the results you desire.

This is a book you can refer to at any time for different issues you want to address in the future—months or even years after you make changes in the initial area(s) of your life. If you have practiced self-hypnosis on a regular basis, you can formulate your suggestions and only do Step 3. If you have not practiced for a month or so, I suggest you go back to Steps 1 and 2 to reestablish the time set. Then refer to the specific chapter that addresses your need now and formulate your suggestions.

When you think about the goals you want to achieve, watch your thoughts.

"Do or do not. There is no try."
—Yoda

"Whether you think you can or think you can't, you're right."
—Henry Ford

Do you know the difference between goals and objectives? Most people think they are the same thing. They are not the same. My definition of a goal is an outcome you want to achieve in a specific time frame. Objectives are the measurable actions or steps you need to take to achieve the goal. For example, your goal may be to lose 20 lb. in six months. Your objectives may be to eat healthier, to start a walking program, and to eat three meals a day. Each of your objectives becomes a self-hypnosis suggestion.

While no one book can cover all issues, I endeavored to address many issues people encounter when coming across the various topics included in this book. You may have an issue related to a topic or topics that has not been addressed. However, I hope I have provided you with enough examples so that you can apply what you have learned to formulate a suggestion for your precise need.

You might want to read Chapter 1, "Just 3 Minutes a Day" after you decide the issue you want to work on. I am your cheerleader, and I want you to succeed.

This is the first book in a series of hypnosis self-help books. Future books expand on different issues such as weight management, stopping smoking, dealing with cancer, and memory and learning. If you want to be notified about future books, go to my website www.joannabrahamsen.com and download a free booklet, *Reprogram Your Subconscious Mind*. You will then be on my mailing list and will receive notifications about future books.

I wish you success as you begin your journey to change your life. All it takes is three minutes a day!

CHAPTER 3

Facts About Hypnosis

I have always been interested in hypnosis ever since I was twelve years old and bought a book advertised on the back of a comic book called *The Key to Hypnotism*. I read the entire book and then went to the library to find more books on hypnotism. I wondered what it would be like to be hypnotized, but it was not until I was on a date and passed a Greenwich Village coffeehouse advertising a hypnosis show by the Great Gardino that I had the chance. When he asked for volunteers, I was one of the first to go up on stage. After we were hypnotized, he gave us the suggestion that our hands were tightly clasped together, and we could not take them apart. I tried, and I could not. I did not "feel" hypnotized and thought I could unclasp my hands anytime, but I did not feel like it. I felt very relaxed, and the feeling lasted for hours.

If you ask ten hypnotists what hypnosis is, you will get at least ten different answers. Hypnosis can be defined as an altered state characterized by extreme suggestibility, relaxation, and heightened imagination. Usually, one person (the hypnotist) talks to another (the subject) in a special way that puts the subject into a trance. I prefer to define hypnosis simply as the bypass of the critical faculty and the establishment of selective thinking. The critical faculty is your conscious mind that analyzes and makes decisions. Selective thinking is the suggestions that you are willing to accept without analyzing. In self-hypnosis, you act as the hypnotist when you give yourself suggestions and as the subject when you accept those suggestions.

But you may ask, "What is hypnosis like?" As you are sitting there reading this book, allow your eyes to close for a moment after reading this sentence. With your eyes closed, you can still hear the sounds around you. Maybe you hear a clock ticking or the sound of the TV or computer. You may be more relaxed because you have eliminated the visual input. That is what hypnosis feels like. You are not "out," "under," "zonked," etc.

We all experience states that are like hypnosis every day. Think about what it is like when you first wake up in the morning. You lie there after waking up from sleep, but you are so comfortable and relaxed, and you are thinking how nice it would be to close your eyes for "just five more minutes." There is also the time at night when you are just drifting off to sleep when you are not quite asleep but not fully awake. These states are like hypnosis.

Do you drive? Walk? Ride public transportation? Have you ever gone from point A to point B and not remembered passing certain landmarks? Maybe you have arrived at your destination and did not know how you got there. But you were not asleep, were you? If you came to a "Stop" sign, you stopped. Or if someone cut you off, you would apply the brake. If you were walking and came to a "Don't walk" sign, you would stop. If you were riding public transportation, you would get off at your stop. These are states like hypnosis. You are always aware of your surroundings, but your conscious mind is occupied with other thoughts, like what to make for dinner, or solving a problem at work, while your subconscious mind controls the car or your footsteps.

Have you ever been so engrossed in a movie, book, or TV show and someone came into the room and asked you a question? Although you were aware they were speaking to you, you either chose not to hear them or, without realizing it, you answered the question and were told later that you did, in fact, speak to them. This is a state like hypnosis where the whole focus of your attention is on the book, movie, or TV show. If you wanted to, you could have answered the person, but you chose not to. Or your subconscious mind answered without you being aware of it. When you are in hypnosis, your subconscious mind is always totally in control.

Hypnosis is nothing new. It is a natural state of awareness that gives you an extraordinary feeling of mental, physical, and emotional relaxation. In this relaxed state, the subconscious mind becomes very receptive to accepting positive, beneficial suggestions. These suggestions are given directly to your receptive, uncritical, subconscious mind, bypassing the critical, conscious signals, which contribute toward continued, undesired behavior such as smoking or overeating.

Hypnosis is a safe, effective modality. It can help you reprogram your computer-like subconscious mind to make incredible changes to empower you to be the master of your conscious mind and behavior.

Hypnosis feels very much like a deep daydream. In hypnosis, your mind is active; your thoughts and actions are under your control; you hear every sound in the room; you can answer questions, and you remember everything that is said. No two people experience hypnosis in the same way, but all agree that being in hypnosis is a very pleasant experience.

Willpower and Habits

There are many undesirable habits that can be modified with hypnosis. Smoking and overeating are two examples. Although most individuals attempt to change their habits with willpower alone, they find it is not enough.

For hypnosis to be most effective, it is essential that you are willing to make a commitment to change, and this commitment must become more powerful than the urge to overeat or smoke. The power of your imagination is used in conjunction with hypnosis, and together you can accomplish goals where willpower alone would and has failed. When imagination and willpower are in conflict, imagination always wins.

Just imagine I have placed a board on the floor in front of you. The board is two feet wide and eight feet long. I ask you to walk from one end of the board to the other. You would be able to do that, would you not? Now I place the same board between two ten-story buildings. Now what? Most of you would not walk across it. Why not? It's the same board. But now your imagination takes over and you think you could fall.

Approaches to eliminating smoking, changing eating habits, or whatever you want to change with hypnotic conditioning depend on your motive for change. You have to be willing to do the work involved to make that change.

11

Myths and Misconceptions

There are numerous misconceptions about hypnosis. The most common misconception is that hypnosis is sleep. Hypnosis is not sleep. In hypnosis, unlike sleep, one hears and responds to instructions and suggestions. Although outwardly hypnosis resembles sleep, the actual state of hypnosis is in no way related to sleep. Some people believe that under hypnosis, you are unconscious or exist in a "zombie" like state. Nothing could be further from the truth. You are always aware of what is going on around you. You will hear everything that is said, and you can even speak under hypnosis should you want to communicate. You can speak, open your eyes, walk around the room, etc. Another common misconception is the hypnotized person will lose control and be under the hypnotist's "spell." Subjects are not dominated by the will of the hypnotist but are in control of themselves, aware of their environment, and always capable of making decisions. Therefore, a hypnotized person asked to commit an action that is objectionable to him would simply reject doing it, and in some cases, a person will awaken from hypnosis. Nor will anyone reveal any secrets during hypnosis.

Finally, the misconception of not waking up is mostly caused by the fact that some individuals like the effects of hypnosis so much that they resist awakening. What would happen if a subject is hypnotized and the hypnotist goes away or even dies? The subject could respond in one of two ways. First, without hearing the hypnotist, the subject will open their eyes and end the hypnosis. Second, the subject will automatically pass from hypnosis into normal sleep and wake up a few minutes later.

Conditions for Hypnosis

There are four basic elements that allow hypnosis to take place:

Belief

Belief is the conviction or acceptance that certain things are true or real. I started my hypnosis training when my son was about three years old. I always spoke in a positive way to him and stressed he could do whatever he set his mind to do in simple language that he could understand. When my son was around five, we went on an "adventure" every Saturday. This one Saturday, we went to a park that I was unfamiliar with. He played on the slide and swings for a while. Then he noticed more playground equipment on a lower level of the park. "I want to go down there," he said.

I looked for a way to get to the lower level, but all I saw was a hilly slope with rocks, bushes, and small trees between us and the lower level. I said to my son, "Mommy can't go down that hill. Mommy will fall."

Anton said, "Mommy, if you believe you can do it, you can do it!" Guess who went down that hill without falling? However, you must be aware of the physical limitations of your beliefs. For example, I told my son that no matter how much he believed he could fly, it was impossible for him to do so. If you want to lift weights, but never lifted weights before, you cannot start to bench press 100 lb., no matter how much you believe you can do it.

You must have the belief you are hypnotizable and that you can learn self-hypnosis easily. In the beginning, if you are learning this on your own, you may not feel that you are hypnotized. This is normal. Just continue to practice the self-hypnosis exercises as they are described in this book.

Attention

Attention is the ability or power to keep the mind focused and to concentrate. Whatever you place your attention on will increase. One of my clients wanted to increase his income. I suggested he formulate suggestions based around investing, decreasing his spending, and getting a better job. Several months after he practiced self-hypnosis, he was offered a promotion at his current job with a substantial increase in salary. The more you practice self-hypnosis, the better you will get. Follow the instructions and focus on what you are doing. However, do not try to be hypnotized. The harder you try to achieve a goal, the more difficult it becomes. Most people do not feel hypnotized at first. Just relax and continue to practice the three steps described later in this book.

Expectation

Expectation is a strong belief that you should achieve something. When I was in college, I answered an ad posted on a bulletin board near the psychology department. "Wanted: College students to test their susceptibility to hypnosis." The ad listed Dr. Peter Field as the contact and a phone number. I called, and a melodious, deep voice answered the phone. I fell in love with the voice and knew I would be a good hypnotic subject. Dr. Field was easily able to hypnotize me. I was an excellent subject. I expected Dr. Field would easily hypnotize me, that I would be a good subject, and that is what happened. This is a strong mechanism of hypnosis. If you expect to hypnotize yourself, you succeed.

Imagination

The ability to form mental images of things that are not present to the senses. This is the most powerful element of hypnosis! Imagine holding a fragrant, juicy lemon in your hand. Notice its color, shape, and size. How does it feel? Smooth? Rough? Cut it open, look inside, and notice its translucent, pale, yellow color. Inhale its aroma. Gently squeeze the lemon. Some of the juice flows. Bite the lemon. Are you salivating? Are you puckering? Why? There is no lemon. The thought of tasting the lemon produced a physical reaction. You were using your imagination. That is how powerful your imagination is. During self-hypnosis, you imagine that you have already stopped smoking, are exercising, or have changed your eating habits.

For hypnosis to be most effective, it is necessary that you are willing to make a commitment to change, and this commitment must become more powerful than the urge to overeat, smoke, remain a couch potato, etc. The power of your imagination is used in conjunction with hypnosis, and together you can accomplish goals where "willpower" alone would and has failed. When imagination and willpower are in conflict, imagination always wins. Eliminating smoking, changing eating habits, or achieving your goals with hypnotic conditioning depends on your motive for change. Because you are going to be formulating your own suggestions in your own words to make the changes you want, you can easily succeed because you will be motivated, and you expect to derive certain benefits from the change.

Uses of Hypnosis and Contraindications

There are many uses of hypnosis: weight control, smoking cessation, stress management, motivation, self-confidence, memory and learning skills, sales and sports performance, public speaking, pain management, childbirth, insomnia, fears, phobias, forensics, regression, and many others, but the best use of self-hypnosis applies to weight control, smoking cessation, stress management, motivation, self-confidence, memory and learning skills, sales and sports performance, public speaking, performance enhancement, and creativity.

Although pain management responds well to hypnosis, you should not ignore the body's warning mechanism. Pain is a symptom of a problem. You may be masking a broken bone or a tumor. Before you use self-hypnosis for any medical or dental concern or use self-hypnosis to eliminate or minimize pain, you should first check with your doctor or dentist.

CHAPTER 4

Self-Hypnosis: Is it for You?

Hypnosis is Safe

Hypnosis and self-hypnosis are safe. A client of mine was extremely nervous about going into hypnosis. I asked the client about their concern. The client mentioned a movie in which the hypnotist put a whole group of people into hypnosis and then had a heart attack. Were the people "stuck" in hypnosis? I explained that if you were put into hypnosis by me or any hypnotist, and there was no interaction between you and the hypnotist after several minutes, you would do one of two things. You would be so relaxed that you might drift off to sleep and wake up a few minutes later feeling refreshed or you would open your eyes and bring yourself out of hypnosis on your own.

When you are doing self-hypnosis, you can bring yourself out of hypnosis at any time. All you need to do is suggest you are emerging from hypnosis and open your eyes. Should a situation arise that requires your attention, if the doorbell or phone rings, you just open your eyes, and you can take care of the situation. You could then choose to go back into hypnosis after you have handled the situation or go back into hypnosis another time. I suggest that before you do your self-hypnosis exercise, you plan to eliminate distractions in the beginning. Turn off the phone, the computer, the radio, or the TV. When I was doing self-hypnosis, my dog, a black lab, sensed my relaxed state and wanted "in." Therefore, I learned to close the bedroom door before I practiced self-hypnosis. If you have children, a spouse, or pets, you should adjust your surroundings so they do not disturb you.

Visualization

When you practice self-hypnosis, you will be imagining yourself making the change. You may say you do not "see" pictures in your mind. Let's do some experiments. Picture your front door. What color is it? Is it solid or does it have glass? What does the doorknob look like? Some people get a picture in their mind, while others get a sense of the door or a feeling. However you imagine the door is correct for you. Want to do another experiment? Close your eyes. Imagine an apple. What color is it? What kind of apple is it? However you "do that" is how you imagine in hypnosis. When you imagine yourself looking in the mirror at your ideal weight, or acing the test, or giving that speech, do the same thing! You will use this powerful imagination of yours to achieve your goal.

Habit

Do you remember when you first learned how to perform a physical skill, such as riding a bike or driving a car? You really had to think about what you were doing. How to hold your hands, how much pressure to apply to the gas or brake pedal. How to balance yourself on the bicycle seat. But once you learned the proper techniques, you did not have to think about those things anymore, did you? The learning became unconscious, and the acts became habits. Whenever you want to change a habit, you must first think about the behavior consciously. Just for a moment, think about which sock you put on first or which shoe you tie first. Now suppose I told you that starting tomorrow you must start with the opposite sock or shoe. Now, when you put on your socks or shoes, what do you have to do? That's right, you must consciously think about the change you are making. In the beginning it is uncomfortable. It takes some time to get used to the change. Performing any behavior that's different is uncomfortable at first. But what happens as you repeat the behavior? It becomes familiar and comfortable.

In psychology, a habit is defined as any regularly repeated behavior that requires little or no thought and is learned rather than innate. There are both healthy habits and unhealthy habits. Looking both ways before crossing the street is a healthy habit. Brushing your teeth is a healthy habit. Biting your fingernails is an unhealthy habit. The good news is that any habit can be changed. However, you must want to change.

Let us perform an experiment. Just for a moment, clasp your hands together in your normal fashion. Maybe you interlock your fingers with your left thumb on top. Good! Now change it. Clasp your hands in a different way. Perhaps your right thumb is now where your left one used to be. Maybe you put one hand inside the other so your right hand is in your left hand. Just change the way you clasp your hands. Good! Now go back to the familiar way. Now go back to the new way. Just for a few moments, switch back and forth between the old way and the new way. Now stop on the new way. How does it feel? Not as uncomfortable now as when you first clasped your hands a different way, is it?

19

You can get used to a new behavior after you consciously practice it for a while. The change has then become unconscious. Your new habit is now part of your current behavior. As you continue to practice your new behavior, it becomes a permanent part of you.

Three Methods of Self-Hypnosis

There are three methods by which an individual can learn self-hypnosis. The first method is the direct posthypnotic suggestion method. In this method, the person is hypnotized by a qualified hypnotist and taught through posthypnotic suggestion how to induce the hypnotic state using a cue, word, or signal. The second method uses a combination of posthypnotic suggestion in conjunction with training the person to enter hypnosis using self-hypnosis suggestions and this method is practiced under the hypnotist's supervision until some degree of self-hypnotic control is achieved. In the third method, the person learns to hypnotize themself by reading about the technique and applying the methods.

I believe that the self-hypnosis method, as outlined in this book, helps you achieve the best results because when you enter hypnosis, your conscious critical mind rests, allowing the subconscious mind, the part of you where changes are made come to the forefront. With other methods, after you enter hypnosis, you then think of suggestions to give yourself. You are using your conscious mind, and you lighten the hypnotic state. With my method, because you give yourself suggestions before you enter hypnosis, your subconscious mind can totally focus and concentrate on the suggestion itself without the conscious mind slowing it down. While you can achieve results with other methods, I believe you can achieve results faster with my method of self-hypnosis.

I want to thank the National Guild of Hypnotists for permission to reprint the 3-Step Self-Hypnosis procedure outlined in the NGH Certification Training with credit given to Dr. Richard Harte and the National Guild of Hypnotists—www.NGH.net— in this book. I teach this method of self-hypnosis to my clients and students.

CHAPTER 5

Self-Hypnosis Step 1: Pre-sleep Technique

When you imagine yourself getting better and better, think about the change you want to make using self-hypnosis. Imagine a slimmer and trimmer you, wearing clothes you love. Imagine yourself a nonsmoker breathing clean, fresh air. Imagine yourself hitting the golf ball perfectly and the ball landing exactly where you want it to go. If you sleep alone, you can either say the suggestion to yourself or out loud. If you sleep with a partner, you should say the suggestion to yourself. Continue Step 1 for a week. You then can move on to Step 2. When you move on to Step 2, you continue to do Step 1.

Instructions for Step 1

1. When you go to bed, starting tonight and continuing for the next seven days, just before you are ready to fall asleep, give yourself the following suggestion ten times:

   "Every day in every way, I get better and better."

   While you are saying the suggestion, imagine yourself in any way you can, getting better and better.

2. In order not to fall asleep and not to lose count, every time you say the suggestion, press down with each finger of your right hand. Then continue with each finger of your left hand until you have completed the suggestion ten times.

3. This may be your first attempt at learning to effectively program yourself through suggestion. It is of the utmost importance to do this exercise every night without falling asleep until you have completed the ten repetitions.

4. You are beginning to establish a habit pattern of properly programming yourself by giving yourself positive suggestions before going to sleep. The next day, you will find yourself reacting very positively to that suggestion.

CHAPTER 6

Self-Hypnosis Step 2: Induction

When you move on to Step 2, you continue to do Step 1 as outlined above. However, you can allow yourself to fall asleep while you are saying, "Every day in every way, I am getting better and better." I suggest you do Step 2 in a comfortable chair, sitting up. Some people lie down, but in this position, the subconscious mind is conditioned to fall asleep, and you will become so relaxed that you may fall asleep. Also, as stated earlier, eliminate distractions as best you can.

Instructions for Step 2

1. Continue doing Step 1, the pre-sleep technique you learned last week. In addition, you are to do the following:
2. Twice a day—once in the morning or at noon, and once in the early evening—you will hypnotize yourself, stay in hypnosis for approximately three minutes, and then wake yourself up. Here's how:
3. Sit in a comfortable chair with your back supported. Focus your attention—effortlessly—on a spot opposite you, slightly above eye level. Take three deep breaths—

slowly—as you count backward: 3 ... 2 ... 1. Close your eyes, exhale, RELAX, and allow yourself to go into a deep, sound, hypnotic rest. You are to remain in hypnosis for approximately three minutes by counting backward slowly from fifty (50) to one (1). Note: It will help if you allow yourself to visualize or imagine each number being written on a movie, computer, or TV screen as you count backward.

4. To awaken, just count forward from one to three, and you will awake refreshed and alert, ready to go about your business in an energetic way.

5. Do this exercise twice a day for seven days, after which you will be ready to give yourself helpful and beneficial suggestions.

CHAPTER 7

How to Formulate Suggestions

I had a client who wanted to lose weight. She had a class reunion in ten weeks and wanted to lose 20 lb. and weigh 130 lb. I told her this was doable. I taught her how to formulate suggestions to achieve that goal. I asked her to come back in a week and show me her suggestion. Her suggestion read: In ten weeks, I weigh 130 lb., and I feel proud of myself. I told her that losing weight was her goal, but the suggestions she would give herself had to contain the specific action she needed to take to achieve that goal. I gave her a sample suggestion after asking her what unhealthy habits she developed to put on the weight. One of the unhealthy habits was putting too much food on her plate, and then she felt she had to eat it all. Growing up as a child, her parents would serve her a plate of food and expected her to eat it all because the people in (insert area or country) were starving.

Suggestion

Whenever I eat a meal, I can easily serve myself smaller portions, and it is acceptable to leave food on my plate. I am in control of what I eat, and I feel great.

I understood this situation all too well. When I was about twelve, my father said, "Finish everything on your plate because the people in Italy are *starving." I responded, "So send it to them." My father gave me that look, grabbed my plate, and sent me to my room for the rest of the evening without dinner.*

As we worked together, my client came up with other suggestions that addressed her unhealthy habits. The goal may be to lose weight, but the suggestions should be geared to what you must **do** to achieve that goal.

Before you use self-hypnosis to give yourself suggestions, you must first learn how to formulate the suggestions correctly. The subconscious mind, although capable of great power, is simple and childlike. Because the subconscious mind is unable to reason inductively and lacks a critical faculty, suggestions must be carefully phrased to achieve the desired result. Follow the guidelines below for creating your suggestions.

How to Formulate Suggestions

1. USE ACTION WORDS: The suggestion must include action. You must state what you need to DO to achieve the desired outcome. You must be specific. For example, "I want to relax" may be the suggestion you want to give yourself. It is a good suggestion, but it does not state what you need to do to relax. You are stating the desire or outcome but not the action. A better suggestion would be: "Whenever I want to relax, I take three deep breaths, and I become relaxed." This suggestion includes the specific action you need to take to relax. If you don't include action, then the suggestion is just a wish or desire. You must take action to achieve results.

2. POSITIVE: The suggestion must be positive in tone. Tell yourself what you want to do, not what you want to avoid. When you use negative words, you are reinforcing the undesired

behavior. If I said to you, "Do not think of a pink elephant." What are you thinking of? The subconscious mind does not "hear" the word "not," and it does not like to be told NO! "I do not eat fatty foods" is not a positive suggestion. Under hypnosis, the subconscious mind hears "eat fatty food." The result of a NO is a feeling of deprivation.

In addition to eliminating negative words like "no," "not," "never," etc., you also should avoid words that have negative connotations like "fatty," "unhealthy," "greasy," etc. Even the word "diet" has a negative connotation. You should also avoid words that refer to a condition like "cancer," "asthma," "emphysema," "heavy," "stress," etc. Since you cannot eliminate the word "no" from your mind, you must replace negative words with positive words. A positive suggestion would be, "I eat five servings of fruits and vegetables a day, and I become healthy." Or "I eat those foods that are healthy for me, and I feel great."

Another reason for avoiding negative words is when you are in hypnosis, the words sometimes break up, and you hear "eat...fruits...healthy...feel good...vegetables...healthy." If the words were not all positive what you might hear is "eat fatty foods...foods are unhealthy... eat unhealthily." Which set of words would you prefer? Sometimes it might be necessary to state the problem to take positive action. In those rare instances, you should state the problem (negative) in the past tense and the solution (positive) in the present tense. "Whenever I find myself in a situation that used to cause me to smoke ... I take three deep breaths and relax."

3. SIMPLE: Your suggestion should contain one thought or one idea at a time. You cannot lose weight and stop smoking in the same suggestion. You may want to do both, but you must focus

your attention and your suggestions on one goal at a time. In addition, your suggestion should also be worded plainly. Your subconscious mind is simple. There should be no doubt in your mind what the suggestion is and what the desired outcome is supposed to be. It is necessary for you to clearly understand what is being suggested. The suggestion should only be interpreted in one way. Saying "I eat healthy portions of food" appears to be a good suggestion. But what if your subconscious mind equates "healthy" portions with "large" portions? Correctly stated, it is: "I eat three ounces of chicken and enjoy every bite."

4. BELIEVABLE: This is the most important of all the guidelines. The suggestion must be believable! Believable to whom? It must be believable to you! You must WANT to achieve the results desired. If you do not want to quit smoking, but your doctor says you must, it is unlikely self-hypnosis would work. You also must be gentle with yourself. Your goal may be to exercise every day, but if you start with this suggestion and then miss a day because of illness or bad weather, you will be disappointed and discouraged. You may tell yourself, "What's the use? This hypnosis stuff does not work anyway!" Be patient and go slow. Your suggestion could be, "I walk for ten minutes a day, three days a week, and I feel great!" If you want to walk every day, you can. If you want to walk for twenty or thirty minutes, you can. But if you have never walked as exercise and then suggested to yourself that you walk for thirty minutes every day, is this believable? I had a client who wanted to do aerobics every day for thirty minutes. I asked her how many minutes a day she exercised now. She told me she didn't exercise at all. What are her chances for success if she begins an aerobics class and exercised for even five or ten minutes? She thought she would be exhausted and maybe get hurt.

I offered a better suggestion: "I do aerobics for five minutes a day, three days a week, and I feel great." I told her when the suggestion begins to work, and you are easily exercising five minutes, gradually extend the time limit or increase the number of days you exercise. As you succeed with each small change, each success builds upon each success, and your goal becomes more believable. Gradual changes are more believable!

5. USE PRESENT TENSE: If you give your subconscious mind an excuse to postpone the suggestion, your subconscious mind will comply. A suggestion "I will exercise ..." gives the subconscious permission to wait until tomorrow. Close your eyes for a moment. Imagine yourself "will... walking." You cannot do it, can you? Saying, "I exercise," or "I am becoming fit and trim" allows the subconscious to "see" itself as actually achieving the goal. Seeing yourself performing the action increases the motivation for making the change. You also imagine yourself already enjoying the benefits of the change.

6. CREATE A TIME FRAME: You do not have to be rigid in your schedule, but you must set a reasonable length of time to achieve your goal. There must be a way to measure whether you are doing the suggestion. "I exercise three times a week for thirty minutes each time" seems like a good suggestion. But suppose your week ends on Sunday, and it's now Saturday night, and you haven't exercised at all. Does this mean you now have to exercise three times on Sunday? Or, if you don't exercise, does that mean you have failed? A better suggestion is, "I walk for twenty minutes in the morning every Monday, Wednesday, and Friday, and I feel great." If it is now Monday night and you haven't walked for some reason—bad weather, not feeling well, etc.,— you realize you must walk on an alternative day instead. In addition, with a time frame, you will know if the suggestion is

working or not. There are only two reasons a suggestion does not work:

1. You didn't want to make the change in the first place, or

2. (more likely) The suggestion is not worded properly.

Because it can take up to two weeks for a new habit to be formed, wait at least that long. If you are not performing the action suggested, then examine your suggestion. Did you really want to accomplish what you had suggested? Does the suggestion meet these guidelines? If the answer is no, then you must change your goal or change your suggestion.

7. CARRY A REWARD: Making a change is hard work. The subconscious mind is very lazy, but remember, it's also childlike. You need to satisfy the inner child by giving it a reward. To the adult mind, this is known as, "What's in it for me?" A reward will help motivate you and make it easier for you to act. The reward can be the benefit you hope to achieve from doing this work. For example, "I ride my stationary bike for twenty minutes, three mornings a week on Tuesday, Wednesday, and Saturday, and I look great in my clothes." Or the reward can be as simple as "... and I feel good about myself." What do you want as a reward? Include the reward in your suggestion while feeling and seeing yourself enjoying the reward!

For practice in formulating suggestions, take a piece of paper and write a suggestion about the behavior you want to change or any habits you need to change or eliminate. See the worksheet included in this chapter. Examine your statement in consideration of each of the guidelines. Read your suggestion again. Is there action? Does it express one idea in simple terms? Is the suggestion in the present tense. Is the statement positive?

31

Do you really want to accomplish what you suggested? Does it contain a unit of measurement or time? Is there a reward? Remember, if you are not getting results, examine the suggestion. Make sure it's something that you really want to accomplish, that it's worded properly, and meets all the above guidelines. See the appendix for the Self-Hypnosis Worksheet.

Here is an example of a suggestion that meets all the above criteria:

Suggestion

Every Tuesday, Thursday, and Saturday at 10:00 a.m., I spend twenty minutes putting items away that are on my dining room table and because I have a clear table, I invite friends over to dinner and feel proud of myself.

Let us analyze the suggestion according to the guidelines outlined above, "How to Formulate Suggestions."

- Action: The suggestion describes what she must DO to have a clear dining room table. She spends (time) and (puts away).
- Positive: All the words are positive in tone.
- Simple: One thought—clear the dining room table.
- Believable: At first, she said, "every day" at 10:00 a.m. I asked her was this believable. She agreed to limit the work on those specific days. In addition, she said she would spend an hour. This time frame was not believable, and she settled on twenty minutes.
- Present tense: Spend…put… have…invite.
- Time Frame: The time and days are specific. Come Sunday, and she did not spend those days and times

working on the table, she needs to revise the suggestion to maybe two days a week or maybe ten minutes at a time.

- Reward: She enjoys a clear table and has friends over.

In the chapters that follow, sample suggestions are included. However, you should use these suggestions as a guide. The best suggestions are the ones you make up yourself for your own unique situation.

There are other suggestions throughout this book that meet the criteria in different ways. They will still work. However, it's best you follow the above guidelines for the suggestions to work the best.

CHAPTER 8

Self-Hypnosis Step 3:
Programmed Suggestion

B y this time, you would have done Step 2 for a week, and your subconscious mind will know approximately when three minutes have passed. Do not do Step 3 until you have done Step 2 at least once a day for a week. If you don't, your subconscious mind won't be able to determine when approximately three minutes have passed. Don't be concerned if your elapsed time is not three minutes. For you, the time may be two and a half minutes or even three and a half minutes. Whatever the time set is for you is okay.

1. The third step in self-hypnosis is to be started one week after you complete the exercises for Step 1 and Step 2. Once you start Step 3, you no longer need to do Step 2.

2. For Step 3, you need a 3 x 5 index card, a business card, which can always be easily carried with you, or even your smartphone notes app. You are to write the suggestion you have prepared for yourself which meets the guidelines Action Words, Positive, Simple, Believable, Time Frame, Present Tense, and Carry a Reward.

3. Again, sit down, and choose a spot opposite you, slightly above eye level. Hold the written suggestion in front of the spot and read the suggestion to yourself three times. Make sure the words on the card are BELIEVABLE to you and allow yourself to IMAGINE accomplishing what is written on the card. Use your imagination.

4. You have written your suggestion and have chosen your spot. Read the suggestion to yourself three times. Now put your suggestion down and take your first deep breath. Exhale. Take your second deep breath. Exhale. Now take your third deep breath. Hold it. Close your eyes. Count backward from 3 to 1. Exhale and go deep into hypnosis.

5. At this point, instead of counting backward from 50 to 1, allow the suggestion to repeat over and over in your subconscious mind. At the same time, imagine that you are carrying out the suggestion, and enjoying the rewards.

6. You will find that at times, the words start to break up and become fragmented. That is perfectly okay. The important words or phrases will come through to you.

7. In approximately three minutes, you'll have a feeling that it's time to stop and bring yourself out of hypnosis. (Note: this time was set when you established the habit pattern in Step 2.) At this point, just count forward: 1... 2... 3, open your eyes, come out of hypnosis, feeling refreshed and relaxed in every way. Give yourself time to allow the suggestion to take hold. It can take up to two weeks to start getting the benefits related to your suggestion.

8. NOTE: If you are not getting results, examine the suggestion. Make sure it's something that you really want to accomplish and that it's worded properly, meeting all the above guidelines.

CHAPTER 9

Weight Management

When I participated in my first hypnosis training course in 1986, I was at least 40 lb. overweight. My instructor said, "You want to help others to lose weight. What will they think when they look at you? You are fat!" Insulted at first, I then realized what the instructor said made sense. To help others lose weight, I needed to address my own issues. The instructor taught me self-hypnosis to change the habits that contributed to my being overweight. I have continued to use these techniques to maintain a healthy weight.

Dealing with my weight has been an ongoing issue for me. I was chubby in kindergarten. My father called me "pleasingly plump." As a woman, I was zaftig (Yiddish for having a full rounded figure.) In college, I dieted, and after a year, I fit into a size 14. At age 34, I became pregnant and gained 40 lb. My mother told me not to worry because once the baby was born, I would lose the weight. After the baby was born, I only lost 18 lb. The rest stayed with me. I was a snug size 18. It was at this point that I began hypnosis classes and began to apply self-hypnosis to manage my weight.

Using hypnosis, I lost over 35 lb. While I was at a hypnosis conference in Chicago, I looked at the vendor stalls. I spotted a beautiful royal blue silk dress with black sequins and beads—a size 12. The vendor encouraged me to try it on. I did, and it fit! I was so happy. I wore it that Saturday night to the dinner dance during the conference. The dress was made slightly larger than a size 12; most likely, it was a size 14. I still have it hanging in my closet. I plan to wear it again! Do you have a special item of clothing hanging in your closet? Does it fit now? You can use the visualization in your self-hypnosis session of you wearing the item again at your new size and weight.

This chapter addresses how to lose and manage your weight by applying self-hypnosis techniques to change the habits that cause you to overeat. This chapter does not address those issues where being overweight is the result of physiological or psychological causes. For those issues, you need to seek the advice of a medical professional.

How many times have you rigidly followed a diet until you lost weight? You suffered, your stomach growled, and all you thought about was that you could have the four ounces of carrot juice but not get within twenty yards of a French fry. You accepted this agony as an inevitable part of the weight loss process.

Then finally, you reached your goal. You stopped dieting and started eating normally like you did before you started your diet. Soon, you gained all the weight back. This illustrates the most prevalent factor in unsuccessful weight reduction: The loss of pounds is not permanent when you do not change the habits causing you to overeat. This chapter focuses on those people who overeat and who are not active.

While the subconscious is no simple power to grapple with, it's only through permanent changes in this part of your mind that you will experience permanent changes in your life—changes that come automatically and are not painful. If you can accept the subconscious as your friend instead of your enemy, you will be able to look at what is causing the behavior that makes you unhappy. You must be willing to make a lifestyle change.

I have been teaching a weight management course at a local community college for the last fifteen years. I always ask my class, "Do diets work?" Some participants will answer "Yes," and some will answer "No." I explain that both answers are correct. If you are on a diet, you lose weight, but as soon as you go off the diet, you backslide. In our society, we suffer from "lightbulb thinking." We are either on a diet or off a diet. Even the word "diet" has a negative connotation. And why do we always start a diet on a Monday?

This chapter will not discuss diets. Rather we will address many of the reasons people are overweight and how to change those habits. We will also address incorporating more activity (dare I say, exercise) into your life. The self-hypnosis suggestions that follow will help you identify and change unhealthy habits and help you incorporate healthy eating and increased activity habits.

If you are like me, you have many weight loss books. They address topics such as dealing with emotional issues, low-fat cooking, various diets, and exercise. Most of the diet books agree, though, that people gain weight because they take in more calories than they need, and they do not expend enough energy to lose that weight.

Maybe you need to cook healthier. Maybe you need to get more exercise. Maybe you need to eat slower. At one point in my battle with weight, I was even ready to give up and be okay with being a size 2X. I bought several books with the theme "Big is Beautiful." However, I wanted to look better in my clothes, feel better, and fit again into my favorite jeans and dress clothes again. If you are happy with being larger than what the books say is "normal," then you can skip this chapter. I just caution you to make sure you are in good health and have no medical issues.

Identify the Reason You Overeat

When you identify the reasons you overeat, you can address them with suggestions.

You may eat because you want to be noticed, to gain authority, to command more attention, feel more important, or you may like to take up more space. If this seems farfetched, consider the amount of attention given to anyone who is tremendously overweight—someone you squeeze past in the supermarket aisle, someone who wedges himself in the seat next to you at a play, or someone who overflows in the seat adjoining yours on the airplane.

You may eat when you need love. This statement is difficult. Just substitute "I" for "you." Say, "I eat when I need love." The declaration almost hurts. The more uncomfortable you feel trying this one on for size, the more likely it is to be the cause of your overeating—and it is a perfectly logical cause. Go back to the beginning of your life again. Food was often substituted for love.

You may overeat when you really want someone to give you a kind word, touch you, or give you a hug. You may want someone to make love to you, so you love yourself by giving yourself lots of wonderful things to eat. Sadly, this behavior creates a treacherous cycle: As you create a bigger self, the more likely you will be, from a social point of view, unlovable. Unfortunately, our society rewards thin and scorns fat which leads us to the next major cause.

You may eat because you are afraid. Afraid of what? One common fear is your own sexuality. If you are unattractive to the opposite sex, you do not have to worry about the consequences, problems, opportunities, and decisions a relationship can bring. You can stay in your present situation, which demands nothing of you emotionally or physically because you are not sought after.

One woman artist allows herself to get "up in pounds," as she puts it, because "I don't want to be physically attractive. I don't want to have to worry about it. Men don't seek me out, and I don't have to deal with a relationship. I can devote myself to my work." But is she just afraid of her own emotions?

A husband may encourage his wife to stop for donuts or a hot fudge sundae just when she has just taken off a few pounds. His sabotage will help her quickly gain it back again. Why does he do it? It is his insurance against other male attention.

Another fear may be related to good health. You may have been brought up to believe thin was unhealthy. The message you received growing up may have been, "Plump is healthy. If you are healthy, you are less vulnerable to disease." So you make sure that you always have pounds to spare and thus keep illness at bay.

Let's look at some other reasons people overeat.

Reasons People Are Overweight

Many reasons for overeating have little to do with food. It took me a long time to realize this, so I hope you can learn from my mistakes.

- You eat to reward.
- You eat too fast.
- You eat for "hunger to come."
- You eat to satisfy your emotions.

From the beginning of your life, you have been rewarded with food for anything from a simple task to a monumental success. As a baby, you get a cookie as a reward for "potty training." As a child, you get dessert for cleaning your plate, or at least for eating your Brussels sprouts! You get cookies for practicing your cello. As a teenager, the coach takes your team out for pizza after a good game. At graduation, your parents celebrated at the best restaurant they could afford. It's time to learn about nonfood rewards.

What habits do you need to change and formulate a suggestion around? Do you need to increase your activity? Begin with something simple. Do you have a stationary bike or treadmill that has become a clothes hanger?

You Eat as a Reward

Suggestion

As a reward for accomplishing (achieving) (insert accomplishment), I choose to (insert reward) and I feel great! (or see reward ideas)

Suggestion

I enjoy a piece of fruit as a midday or evening snack, and I take time to read a few pages on my Kindle, and I look good in my clothes.

Sample Accomplishments

- Exercising (treadmill, stationary bike, or other similar) for ten minutes, gradually increasing to thirty minutes.
- Eating smaller portions or reducing treats.

Reward ideas:

- go to the movies or watch TV
- post on social media
- enjoy a bubble bath
- play with my pet
- read a magazine or book
- play a game, do a puzzle
- listen to my favorite music

Always add:

- and I feel great
- I look good in my clothes
- I feel slim and trim . . .

or any appropriate addition.

You Eat Too Fast

When you eat, the body takes at least twenty minutes to register fullness. Eating slowly helps you feel full the moment it happens, not when it's too late.

If you want to eat slower:

- Put the utensils down between each bite.
- Eat with the reverse hand. If you are right-handed, eat with your left hand and vice versa.
- Eat mindfully. Look at the food for a moment before digging in. Notice the assorted colors, textures, smells, and tastes. Savor the food.

Suggestions

- **As I learn to eat slower, I put the utensils down between each bite, I enjoy my food, and I am slim and trim.**
- **If I find myself eating too fast, I switch hands to slow my eating, and I look good in my clothes.**
- **Whenever I eat, I take the time to savor my food, and I feel great every time I look in the mirror.**

You Eat for Anticipated Hunger

Hunger is a physiological signal. Appetite is simply the desire to eat. You can learn to recognize the difference between appetite and hunger. When you feel an emptiness in your stomach, that is a hunger signal. When you pass a bakery and smell the aroma of baking bread, and you go in to buy some bread, that is appetite.

Many people lived through the Depression. They never knew if there would be enough food at the next meal. So they ate more than they needed at the current meal to prepare for doing without. When I was in college, I would have four hours of classes in a row, so before classes started, I would eat, even if I wasn't hungry, to stave off hunger until I had time to eat later. I wasn't hungry, but I might be at some point. It didn't make sense. Only eat when you are hungry. You will not starve. We have an abundance of food. If you have food insecurities, keep an apple or snack bar in your bag. If you are not hungry, do not eat.

Suggestion

I eat only when I am hungry, and I take charge of my eating (or; and I manage my weight, or; and I am in control of all my eating habits.)

Emotional Eating

Emotional eating can sabotage your weight loss efforts. It often leads to eating too much—especially high-calorie foods. This pattern to lessen any unpleasant experience is anchored when you are young. A baby is teething and is miserable, so the baby gets a tasty teething biscuit, the perfect antidote for sore gums. A child falls off a swing, and a well-meaning adult dries the child's tears and gives them a cookie. You don't get accepted to your desired college, get the job, or make the sale, so you go out and binge with friends.

You know which things are so upsetting that they propel you to that cute little bistro around the corner where the fondue is delicious. But how long does the food rush last? If you're honest, you will admit the hurt is only partially desensitized while you devour the cheesecake. You need to find nonfood ways to comfort yourself. If you're prone to emotional eating, you can take steps to regain control of your eating habits.

Tame your stress. Try a stress management technique, such as self-hypnosis, yoga, meditation, or deep breathing.

Suggestion

Whenever I feel stressed, I take three deep breaths, and I feel calm, relaxed, and in control.

Have a hunger reality check. Is your hunger physical or emotional? If you ate a few hours ago, you are not hungry.

Suggestion

I eat only when I am hungry, and I am in control of my eating.

Fight boredom. Instead of snacking, substitute healthier behaviors. Take a walk, watch a movie, play with your pet, listen to music, read, or call a friend.

Suggestion

Whenever I feel bored and don't know what to do, I (take a walk, watch a movie, play with my pet, listen to music, read, or call a friend and (add a reward) I feel great, etc.

- Take away temptation. Don't keep hard-to-resist comfort foods in your home. Postpone trips to the grocery store until your emotions are in check. If you live with others who want snacks, put the snacks in a place where you won't see them.
- Don't deprive yourself. When you limit calories and banish treats, you may increase cravings. Eat satisfying amounts of healthier foods, enjoy an occasional treat, and eat a variety of foods to help curb cravings.
- Snack healthy. Choose healthy snacks such as fresh fruit, vegetables with low-fat dip, nuts (a small handful), or unbuttered air-popped popcorn. Try low-calorie versions of your favorite foods.

Suggestion

Whenever I have a snack, I choose healthy snacks, such as fresh fruit, vegetables with low-fat dip, nuts (a small handful), or unbuttered air-popped popcorn and I feel satisfied.

Handling Social Situations

You get promoted to sales manager, and you celebrate by going out to dinner. You take prospective clients out to lunch. You go on a much-needed vacation with your overworked, neglected body, and the first thing you do is seek out those great little restaurant "finds."

You can handle all these situations with new habits firmly established in your friendly subconscious. In fact, you can go to any food-focused function and enjoy being there.

There are plenty of strategies to help you stay on track. You can eat out and not overeat. Order a salad and an appetizer. Start with a clear broth soup. Skip the bread and butter. Most restaurants' portions are large enough for two. You could share an entrée, order an appetizer as a main course, or order an entrée and take half home. Obtain a takeout container and remove half the portion before you start eating. If you must have dessert, order one and split it. Alcohol adds calories. Order mineral water or seltzer instead.

Suggestion

Whenever I go out to eat, I get a take-out container and place half my food in it, (or choose another strategy above) and I feel in control of my eating habit (or other reward).

Handling Buffets

My husband and I love to cruise. We want to enjoy all that the cruise has to offer, including the delicious food. Because we know we're going to allow ourselves to eat more than we usually do, for several months before the cruise, we apply self-hypnosis to help us lose 5 to 10 lb. and we can then indulge without the guilt. You do know, however, that the salt air shrinks your clothes, don't you? LOL!

We usually enjoy going to the buffets for lunch—so much to choose from and such a variety. How can you handle buffets? Look at all the choices and decide before you get in line what you are going to eat. Choose a small portion of protein, a small portion of carbohydrates, and substantial portions of veggies. Choose fruit for dessert or choose one dessert and split it or only eat half.

Suggestion

Whenever I go to a buffet, I choose a small portion of protein, a small portion of carbohydrates, a substantial portion of veggies, and fruit for dessert, and I am in control of my eating habits.

Suggestion

With so many choices available, a buffet is an opportunity to practice my skill to make good food choices.

Increasing Activity

According to the CDC, regular physical activity is important for good health, and it's especially important if you're trying to lose weight or maintain a healthy weight. When losing weight, more physical activity increases the number of calories your body uses for energy or "burns off." The burning of calories through physical activity, combined with reducing the number of calories you eat, creates a "calorie deficit" that results in weight loss. Most weight loss occurs because of decreased caloric intake. However, evidence shows the only way to maintain weight loss is to be engaged in regular physical activity.

Some Ways to "Sneak" in More Activity

- If you work in an office building with stairs, take the elevator one floor below your work floor and walk up the stairs. Gradually increase the stairs by taking the elevator two flights below where you work, etc.

- Park your car a little further from the destination and walk the extra distance.

- If you sit a lot at your job, get up and walk around. Go to the restroom on a different floor and take the stairs. Walk in the hallway for a few minutes. After lunch, take a walk.

- While watching television, get up during commercials and walk around. Do some jumping jacks.

- Stand more. If you usually do an activity sitting down, stand instead. Pace while talking on the phone.

Suggestion

Every day, when I get to work, (insert a different situation), I can easily walk up a flight of stairs (insert any other activity), and I feel energetic.

Increasing your activity on vacation can be a challenge. You need to plan. You can become more active by choosing activities such as swimming, snorkeling, and exploring local cities via walking tours.

Suggestion

While on vacation, I choose a walking tour to explore the city (horseback riding, swimming), and I feel fit and trim.

Drinking More Water

According to the CDC, getting enough water every day is important for your health. Drinking water can prevent dehydration, a condition that can cause unclear thinking, result in mood change, cause your body to overheat, and lead to constipation and kidney stones. Water isn't just "good for you"—water burns fat. Water suppresses hunger. Water renews your skin. You'll also have more energy and save your kidneys and liver from chronic overwork.

A hungry feeling is often mistaken for needing water. Whenever you have a feeling of hunger, drink some water.

Suggestion

Whenever I feel hungry, before I eat something, I take several sips of water, and I am satisfied.

Buy a water bottle with ounces marked on the side. Get an app on your phone to help you keep track of the water you drink. Keep a water bottle in the car and take a sip whenever you come to a red light.

Suggestion

Every time I look at my watch (or other action that you repeat often), I take a sip of water, and I feel more energetic.

Suggestion

Every time I stop at a red light, I take a sip of water, and I feel more energetic.

Other Hints

Read food labels. Note the calories in a serving size. At the beginning of your habit modification, weigh and measure the food. Stick to serving sizes. Three ounces of meat is about the size of a deck of cards, and five ounces of fish is about the size of a checkbook.

Reprogramming for Results

Give less importance to food as it relates to your well-being. Build your confidence so you can accept a slimmer self. Reflect on all the positive things in your life, the goals, and successes you have already achieved, and know that you will continue to be successful. Increase the appeal of healthful foods. Imagine a table in front of you laden with healthful foods that you enjoy anyway; good healthy foods, foods that contain fewer calories, such as _____. You will finish the sentence by inserting the names of the low-calorie foods you most enjoy.

Incorporate new patterns of behavior into your life regarding times, places, and reasons for overeating. "I now have new ways of dealing with my old habits." "When I am _____, I _____." Be sure to include a new option for each issue you have a problem with.

Suggestion

I eat the correct and reasonable amounts of food, and I am totally satisfied. I am satisfied from one meal to the next" and "I am relaxed and peaceful, and food is less and less important."

Suggestion

I create the most healthy and positive life for myself, and I feel great.

Where Do You Go from Here?

Regardless of the cause of your overeating, the procedure you follow for change will be the same. You need to replace the emotional satisfaction that food provides with an activity that serves the same purpose. For example, during a busy day, you may need to stop and take a break. A snack might help you relax, but what you really need at this moment is an appealing, satisfying alternative, such as sitting down, closing your eyes for five minutes and listening to soothing music, or practicing your self-hypnosis, taking three deep breaths, or taking a walk around the block.

You have choices. You can continue to practice those habits that cause you to overeat or change those habits by practicing self-hypnosis and incorporate the suggestions you need the most.

Just remember, it can take two to three weeks for a new habit to form. Take it slow and have patience. Forgive yourself if you slip up. And then get right back on track.

Good luck.

CHAPTER 10

Stop Smoking

"I*t's been* ONE YEAR *since I quit smoking. I have not had a cigarette, cigar, or pipe since we had our session together. You can put me in your success stories. I'm so happy! My wife, on the other hand, is still smoking. You were right when you said you must be ready to quit.*" *This was the message I found on my answering machine from Gary, a stop-smoking client I saw several years ago. He quit; his wife didn't. However, six months after Gary left me this message, his wife came to see me. She wanted to become pregnant, and she was now motivated to quit. We had two sessions, and she quit. A few months after she quit, she became pregnant.*

You have turned to this chapter because you have decided smoking is bad for you. You already know that cigarette smoke contains carcinogens that damage your health. You know that secondhand smoke affects all the people you meet. This chapter will explain how you can use self-hypnosis to quit smoking once and for all. You are the one in control of your habit. You may have tried to quit before. No matter how many times you tried to quit, I believe with the help of self-hypnosis, you can quit for good.

"I don't want to quit smoking altogether. I just want to cut down to three cigarettes a day," said one of my clients, who happened to be a pastor of a local church. He didn't want to quit smoking entirely at first. He was smoking two packs of cigarettes a day at the time. He knew his urge was strongest after finishing a meal, so he wanted to cut down to three cigarettes a day—one after breakfast, one after lunch, and one after dinner. I told him that I believed it was easier to quit altogether instead of cutting down, but as the client wanted, I worked with him over a period of three weeks so he could gradually withdraw and be down to just three cigarettes a day. So, Monday came, and he was smoking three cigarettes a day, and he was happy.

I got a call from him the following Monday. He said, "I messed up. On Saturday, I smoked five cigarettes." I asked him what was different with the Saturday routine. He then shared with me that on Saturdays, he wrote his sermon for Sunday. When he wrote, he paced, and when he paced, he smoked. I asked him if he was successfully smoking only three cigarettes from Sunday to Friday, and he said yes. He was terribly upset at what he considered to be a failure. I told him it was okay if he smoked five cigarettes on Saturday as he was successful all the other days in smoking only three. I congratulated him. Like a little kid, he wanted to know if it was okay to continue to smoke five cigarettes on Saturday, and I answered with a resounding "Yes!" He was relieved. A few months later, he returned for a session to quit smoking altogether. The reverend is now a nonsmoker.

Remember, you are the one who is in control. You decide if you want to quit gradually or all at once. I believe it's easier to quit smoking all at once or "cold turkey." This chapter addresses how to quit NOW!

To succeed at anything, you need a plan. You've got to prepare to quit, plan to quit, quit, and then stick with it. A good strategy makes the difference between success and failure. These strategies work. They have brought success to those who worked the program consistently. Remember, it takes two to three weeks to form a new habit. At first, being a nonsmoker may seem unnatural, but soon it will become easy and comfortable. By practicing the strategies in this chapter for thirty days, you will become and remain a nonsmoker forever.

Decide to Quit

Select the day you will quit. Picking a date too far away gives you time to change your mind or become less motivated. Choose a date that is no more than a week or two away. Let your family and friends know how they can support you.

Do you smoke because you think it relaxes you? Nothing could be further from the truth. When you smoke, your heart rate increases. Does that first inhale feel good? You can have the same effect with deep breathing.

Deep breathing has been used for centuries to calm and relax people. Smokers take a relaxation break every time they light up. When you become a nonsmoker, however, you can keep taking your relaxation breaks and use deep breathing to calm you down. Try the following whenever you feel stressed:

1. Sit in a comfortable chair (or you can do this while standing in line or waiting at a traffic light in the car).

2. Place your hand over your stomach to feel the extension (breathing in) and contraction (breathing out).

3. Breathe in deeply and slowly, then exhale, letting your muscles go limp. Repeat three times.

When you feel the proper expansion and contracting of your diaphragm, you no longer need to place your hand on your stomach.

Suggestion

Whenever I take three deep breaths, I immediately become calm, relaxed, and in control.

Did you know that Ellen DeGeneres quit smoking with hypnosis? Ellen, a longtime smoker, was hypnotized on TV by the legendary Paul McKenna to overcome her smoking habit. Paraphrasing Ellen, "Stopping smoking was the best thing I could do for myself."

No matter how many times you have tried to quit before or if this is your first-time quitting, you have to want the benefits of being a nonsmoker more than the "pleasures" of smoking. Decide now what your benefits are to being a nonsmoker. Do you want a longer life, breathe cleaner air, be a good example for your kids, be able to walk, run, exercise without getting winded, and save money? What are YOUR benefits?

Prepare to Quit

Why Do You Want to Quit?

People who quit successfully are very aware of what they want MORE than they want a cigarette. You must be highly motivated to quit, and you must be confident in your ability to do it. Before you quit, it's important to know why you're doing it. Quitting smoking now improves your health and reduces your risk of heart disease, cancer, lung disease, and other smoking-related illnesses.

List Some of the Benefits You Will Enjoy as a Nonsmoker

On a blank sheet of paper, write down all the benefits that will be yours as a nonsmoker. Some of the benefits many of my clients have listed are:

- Improves your sense of taste and smell; eating will be more enjoyable.
- Will help you feel more energetic almost immediately. Fitness, endurance, and athletic performance will improve.
- Gives you extra money in your pocket.
- Improves your health and the health of your family.
- Breathing is easier, lung capacity will increase, and circulation will improve.
- Stops you from having to worry about where you can "sneak" your next cigarette—no more dealing with the no-smoking laws.
- The house will smell clean and fresh.

If you are having trouble listing your benefits, ask yourself these questions:

- What do I dislike about smoking?
- What do I miss out on when I smoke?
- How is smoking affecting my health?
- What will happen to me and my family if I keep smoking?
- How will my life get better when I quit?

Then write down your reasons and/or benefits for quitting and keep the list with you.

If you still need a reason or reasons to quit, listed here are some of the effects of smoking on the body.

Inhaling tobacco smoke causes damage to many of the body's organs and systems. Some of the effects are as follows:

- Throat irritation leading to coughing and wheezing
- hoarseness
- shortness of breath
- increased blood pressure and heart rate
- reduced blood flow to fingers and toes, sometimes causing cold and/or numb fingers and toes
- increased risk of heart attack and stroke
- greater susceptibility to infections such as colds and flu
- lower levels of protective antioxidants such as vitamin C
- reduced bone density
- reduced ability to smell and taste
- premature wrinkling of the skin
- gum disease

Know Your Triggers

Identify the reasons you smoke. Many say they smoke because of stress, boredom, or habit. Triggers are specific persons, places, or activities that make you feel like smoking. Some common triggers are getting in the car, talking on the phone, solving a problem, having a cup of coffee or tea, after a meal, after sex, or even after exercise. Have a plan for the triggers. For example, when you get the urge, take three deep breaths. If the urge is still there, drink a glass of water and change the activity. You may experience cravings to smoke. Every craving is temporary and having healthy ways to distract yourself can help them fade more quickly.

Plan ahead with a list of activities you can do when you have the urge to smoke, such as calling a friend or taking a walk. What other choices can you make instead of smoking? I call these coping techniques. Formulate your suggestions around your triggers and your coping techniques. Do you smoke after meals? Brush your teeth or pop a mint to get rid of the association between finishing a meal and the taste of a cigarette. Take a walk. Do you smoke in the car? Instead, listen to the radio, pop a hard candy, or put a swizzle stick in your mouth. After making love? Cuddle with your mate instead. Talking on the phone? Pace instead or doodle. Watching TV? Suck on a piece of candy, knit, crochet, or any other activity to occupy your hands. After he retired from football, Rosey Grier took up crocheting and needlepoint to keep his hands busy. If you associate drinking a cup of coffee with a cigarette, maybe you can substitute tea, herbal tea, or juice. Or, while you are drinking coffee, eat breakfast, read the newspaper, a book, magazine, go online or otherwise distract yourself.

Suggestion

Whenever I have the urge to smoke (i.e., after a meal, driving in a car, talking on the phone, or another trigger), I (brush my teeth, listen to the radio, pop a mint, pace, doodle (or another coping technique) and I become a fresh air breather, I smell clean and fresh, I am proud of myself (or another benefit or feeling).

Dealing with other triggers:

What else can you do when you answer the phone other than smoke? You can pace, doodle, chew gum, anything to keep you from lighting up. Other substitutes for cigarettes: swizzle sticks, gum, hard candy, cinnamon sticks, and especially munching on fresh fruit and vegetables.

Suggestion

Whenever I (trigger; finish a meal, talk on the phone, etc., I (activity; take a walk, call a friend, pop a mint) and the urge to smoke passes and I (benefit; jog easily, become long-winded, become a fresh air breather).

Formulate your suggestions around the benefits of being a nonsmoker.

Use your reasons for quitting as one of your suggestions.

I am a nonsmoker because I want _____.

I am a nonsmoker because I want to be able to play with my kids.

Suggestions

I am calm and focused while I drink my morning coffee. I am relaxed, and all I need is coffee.

Whenever I take three deep breaths, I immediately become calm, relaxed, and in control of my habit.

Whenever I drink a glass of water, the urge to smoke passes, and I am a nonsmoker.

When I wake up in the morning, I take several sips of water, and I feel refreshed.

Imagine

Vividly imagine going through your daily routines as a nonsmoker a month from now. You wake up, eat, get ready for work, drive, are at work, relax at home, talk on the phone, and watch TV—all as a nonsmoker. Water sits where the ashtray used to be. The car, your clothes, hair, and breath smell clean. Imagine people congratulating you. Next, imagine yourself in three months' time. You are still a nonsmoker, feeling healthier and more energized each day. Then imagine yourself six months from now, still enjoying being a nonsmoker. Finally, imagine yourself a year from now, celebrating a full year of greater health and vitality, all because you made the decision to stop smoking and stuck by it.

Identify as a Nonsmoker

Identify as a nonsmoker and with people who have successfully quit. You will find yourself automatically behaving AS IF it is true. If others have done it, so can you.

Claim Your Power

Remember other successes you have had in your life—things that may have taken some work, commitment, or persistence. Maybe it was a job, getting through school, learning something new, giving birth, raising children, becoming sober. If you could do that, you can get the cigarettes out of your life once and for all. Look at how small a cigarette pack is. Notice how big your foot is and how nicely the pack fits under your foot. Crush that habit now!

Tell yourself often: "I can do this. I can do anything that I make up my mind to do."

Relax and Breathe

Take three slow, deep breaths whenever you need to relax, relieve stress, or clear away negative thoughts and emotions. Practice breathing to a slow count of 6, 8, or 10 and then exhaling to the same slow count. Do several rounds for instant relief.

Handling Stress

Many people who go back to smoking after they successfully quit do so because of stress. It may be due to a loss—the loss of a loved one, the loss of a job, the loss of a pet. . . You used to smoke to cope with stress. Now you need to learn new coping skills: i.e., self-hypnosis, deep breathing, exercise, taking a walk, meditation, prayer, talking things out with a friend, partner, or significant other, creating a support group, and talking to yourself as you would to your best friend. Keep your mind off cigarettes with distractions. Don't try NOT to think of smoking. Just think of something else. Stay out of your usual smoking places until you feel secure as a nonsmoker. Stay out of bars, away from cigarette machines, or any place where smokers gather.

Drink Lots of Water

Water washes the nicotine out of your body. The physical addiction to nicotine can last anywhere from three days to two to three weeks. This is different for everyone. Drinking lots of water washes the toxins from your body. Aim for six to eight eight-ounce glasses of water a day. Put water where the ashtrays had been. Drink water at those times that you used to smoke, i.e., answer the phone and have a glass of water, finish your meal with a glass of water, drink water in the car.

Suggestion

Whenever I (answer the phone, etc.) I (take a sip of water, pace, doodle, chew gum, etc.) and feel (calm, satisfied, etc.), and I am proud to be a nonsmoker (or another benefit).

Watch your thoughts.

> "Do or do not, there is no try."
> —Yoda

> "Whether you think you can or think you can't, you're right."
> —Henry Ford

Practice thought stopping and switching. Any thought that you allow to stay in your mind will tend to become true. Any words or statements that you regularly express will also tend to come true. You will either talk yourself into or out of success by your speech—spoken aloud or in your mind—as your own worst enemy or best friend. If you think, "I can't do this," you will prove yourself correct. But if you say, "I can do this. I choose to do this because it's the most important thing I can do for my health," you will also prove yourself correct.

If you say that you are "trying" to quit, you sabotage your efforts because "try" implies effort without success. When you are quitting, say, "I AM a nonsmoker on _____ (date)."

Do this exercise. Put a pen or pencil down in front of you. Have it? Good! Now **try** to pick up the pen or pencil. You picked it up, didn't you? I said TRY to pick it up. Trying to pick it up results in an attempt to pick it up, so you DON'T pick it up.

NEVER Just One

Once you quit, never have "just one" again.

Tobacco is addictive. Don't even think that you can smoke occasionally. Few people have ever been able to do that. Just one puff can retrigger your addiction, even if it's been years since you last smoked. Remember what it took to be a nonsmoker and how much better you feel. Don't throw it all away just because you're bored, lonely, upset, or the people around you are smoking. After you have "just one," you will still be bored, lonely, or upset. AND you will have your smoking habit back again to make it all worse.

Final Thoughts

By focusing instead on how your life will be better by not smoking, you will become more excited and more ready to let go.

You pay twice for cigarettes. Once when you get (buy) them and twice when the cigarettes get you.

All benefits are lost if you smoke just ONE cigarette. There is no such thing as an occasional cigarette.

Good luck.

CHAPTER 11

Stress Management

My client's wife was planning a trip to an amusement park. The visit was two weeks away. She planned on riding several roller coasters and wanted my client to go on with her. My client wasn't too keen on the idea. He was fearful of the rapid descent. So, in addition to helping my client handle the job stress, I was able to help him get over his stress about riding the roller coaster. I gave my client a self-hypnosis suggestion he was to use at least once a day before he went on it.

Suggestion

As I ascend the roller coaster, my excitement begins to build, and as I ride the roller coaster, I enjoy the ride.

She was thrilled and excited; he was nervous and stressed. Since he loved his wife and wanted to please her, he was able to reframe his stress into excitement with my help and a self-hypnosis suggestion. So, he rode the roller coaster. He survived and told me later he was happy to have faced his fears and ridden with her.

We all experience stress. It's a part of life. Stress is inevitable if you are alive. Even high levels of stress from serious illness, job loss, a death in the family, or a painful life event such as divorce, is a natural part of life. You may feel down or anxious, and that's normal too for a while. However, if you feel down or anxious for several weeks, you should talk to your doctor. This chapter is not intended to help you deal with serious issues. This chapter will help you with much of the stress that comes with everyday living.

Our bodies are wired for a fight or flight response. Our ancestors had to choose whether to stay and fight or flee. When we're stressed, our bodies produce the hormone cortisol, which gets the body ready to fight or flee. Today, we don't necessarily have to fight or flee, but the body doesn't know that and dumps cortisol into our system. When we don't have to fight or flee to "use up" the cortisol, the hormone accumulates, which leads to "dis-ease," or the absence of ease.

Stress can help motivate you, or it can devastate you. Stress is a feeling of emotional or physical tension that can come from any event or thought that makes you feel frustrated, angry, or nervous. Stress is your body's reaction to a challenge or demand. In short bursts, stress can be positive, such as when it helps you avoid danger or meet a deadline. However, if the stress is constant, it is damaging to your body and mind.

There is both positive and negative stress—good and bad stress. The difference between the two lies in the way you perceive and handle each situation. Shakespeare wrote, "There is nothing either good or bad, but thinking makes it so." Good stress can come from looking forward to an event— a new baby, a promotion, etc. The type of stress is a result of how you perceive the event. My client's wife was excited to ride the roller coaster. My client was stressed. We used self-hypnosis to reframe and convert the stress into excitement. He wanted to change because he loved his wife and wanted to please her. He was motivated to change.

This chapter will not delve deep into what stress is. There are many books and websites that go into the science of stress. What I will do is suggest some coping suggestions to use in various stressful situations you may find yourself in.

What situation(s) triggers your stress? What is your response? You can't control the trigger, but you can control your response. You can mix and match different techniques and responses. You need to formulate your suggestions around the situation or trigger and practice your response to the event during your self-hypnosis session so you can immediately use the self-hypnosis suggestion to cope with the situation.

Deep breathing has been used for centuries to calm and relax people. To practice deep breathing:

1. Sit in a comfortable chair.
2. Place your hand over your stomach to feel the extension (breathing in) and contraction (breathing out); imagine you have a balloon in your stomach, and you're inflating it first before the breath goes into your lungs.
3. Breathe in deeply and slowly, counting from 1–5, then exhale slowly, counting from 1–8. Repeat three times.

When you feel the proper expansion and contracting of your diaphragm, you no longer need to place your hand on your stomach.

Suggestion

Whenever I take three deep breaths, I immediately feel calm, relaxed, and in control.

Repeat this suggestion a couple of times a day for at least a week so you can use this immediately whenever a trigger presents itself.

3, 2, 1 Stress Reducer

Do you want a technique to immediately reduce stress? A colleague of mine, Dr. Richard Nongard, has his clients practice what he calls the 3, 2, 1 Anxiety Reset Technique. I call it the 3, 2, 1 Stress Reducer.

3 deep breaths (see above).

2 hands. Take your right hand and place it on your left shoulder. Take your left hand and place it on your right shoulder. Now hug yourself.

1 minute. Close your eyes for one minute. Notice your breath. Notice how the chair feels beneath you. Notice the sounds around you. Open your eyes. Do not be concerned when one minute has passed.

Driving Can Be Stressful

The husband of a friend of mine would get very upset if someone cut them off in traffic when his wife was driving. The husband would flip them the bird. My friend would get upset at her husband, afraid that the other driver would retaliate against her as the driver. So, while the husband allowed the emotion of anger to control his response, his wife, who had learned self-hypnosis from me, would just take three deep breaths and continue to drive.

Suggestion

Whenever I drive and (trigger; someone cuts me off, speeds ahead of me, drives too slowly), I take three deep breaths, becoming calm and relaxed, and arrive at my destination safely.

Reframing is another technique you can use in any situation. Reframing is expressing a situation differently. Most people see situations in a negative way. Reframing is turning the situation around and expressing it in a positive way. In the above situation, you may think that the driver is cutting you off, speeding past you unsafely, passing a red light, or in any way driving unsafely. Reframe. Think of the situation differently. Maybe his boss told him that if he's late for work one more time, he's fired. Or, if she doesn't get to the appointment on time, she may lose the sale. You reframe by thinking of a positive reason they would perform the action.

Suggestion

Whenever I drive and (trigger; someone cuts me off, speeds ahead of me, etc.) I think that (they may be fired, lose the sale, etc.), and I take three deep breaths and feel calm, relaxed, and in control.

The easiest and quickest way to respond to any trigger is to learn deep breathing in advance of your need to use it. Practice deep breathing several times a day. Then whenever you encounter a trigger, you use the self-hypnosis suggestion below. This suggestion is repeated throughout this book as it's a great technique for almost any situation.

Suggestion

Whenever I need to relax, I take three deep breaths and feel calm, relaxed, and in control.

Other Ways to Reduce Stress

Nature

Take a walk outside. Studies have shown that walking outdoors reduces stress, lowers blood pressure, and improves mood. There are many studies proving that a twenty-minute walk in nature releases endorphins, the feel-good hormone.

Interact with Your Pet

Having a pet to interact with has been proven to lower blood pressure, help you relax, and reduce stress.

Our cat, Nutmeg, will sense when I'm feeling out of sorts or stressed. She'll come over to where I am and rub her head against my hand, so I pet her. The simple act of petting her lets me take a break from whatever I'm doing and helps me relax. My father had an aquarium filled with many kinds of fish. As a young girl, I'd sit in front of the tank and just watch the fish. This activity (or inactivity) would relax me.

Exercise

Stress causes the muscles to tense. Any exercise that causes the muscles to relax is good exercise. Always check with your doctor before you begin an exercise program. Walking, whether on a treadmill or outside, is an exercise most everyone can do. Any exercise that increases your heart rate and your rate of breathing and involves constant movement for twenty to thirty minutes is called aerobic exercise. Do you sit at a desk all day? Check

YouTube or the internet for exercises such as shoulder rotation, overhead stretch, forward bend, neck rolls, and side stretch.

Suggestion

Whenever I feel (stressed, uptight, my muscles tense), I take (three deep breaths, a walk, practice the 3, 2, 1 stress reduction technique, practice neck rolls, shoulder rolls, etc.). I feel the tension leave my body, and I am relaxed.

Humor

As I'm sitting on the radiation treatment table, there are five or six people all looking at me—all either doctors, physicians' assistants, nurses, or technicians—and the results of the breast scan to determine how and if they should give me a boost radiation treatment. I wasn't stressed so much as to the need to have a radiation boost as I was with all these people staring at my half-naked body. And so I quipped, "Well, at least allow me sell tickets, so I can earn some money with all of you standing around looking at me."

Watch a funny movie, a funny YouTube video, read a joke book, go on the internet, or even ask Alexa to tell you a joke. Laughter releases endorphins and oxytocin in your brain, so you feel good after a hearty laugh.

Using Color or an Item as an Anchor to Feel Calm

A colleague's client felt stressed whenever she was walking outside and had to come to a stop, such as a red "Don't walk" sign. She told my colleague that blue has a calming effect on her.

Suggestion

Whenever I see, hear, or perceive the color blue, I immediately feel calm, released, and in control.

So, when she had to stop walking, she sang or hummed to herself songs with the color blue in it, such as "Blue Moon," "Blue Christmas," "Blue Suede Shoes," etc. You get the idea.

Some people have a stone, coin, or other item they carry with them that, when touched, triggers a relaxing response. You can use self-hypnotic suggestion to anchor that.

Suggestion

Whenever I see or feel (insert your token) I immediately feel calm, released, and in control.

Job Stress

A client of mine worked for a tyrannical boss. If my client made a mistake or even if she got called into the boss's office, she would tremble with fear. Many times, her boss would just ask why she handled a client the way she did or just wanted her to explain why she handled a situation the way she did. But sometimes, he would yell at her because she made a mistake. So instead of going into his office in fear and trepidation, she would rehearse in her mind using self-hypnosis how she would handle different situations prior to going to work.

If she was called in to explain a mistake, she would take three deep breaths, before going into the boss's office and calmly explained what she did, why she did it, and offering to correct the mistake immediately.

Rehearsal technique: if you know what situation you are going to be in over and over, you can rehearse your response during your self-hypnosis session.

Other Stress Management Techniques

- Progressive Relaxation
- Autogenic training
- Yoga
- Meditation

You can find these and other techniques on the internet.

Conclusion

Everyone responds to stress in a different way. While you cannot eliminate stress from your life, you can control your response to stress and those triggers you encounter. You have choices. You can change the situation, i.e., find another job, change your thinking, respond to stress in a different way, and/or learn coping skills such as self-hypnosis and other techniques to handle stressful situations.

CHAPTER 12

Miscellaneous Applications: Changing Habits

Nail Biting

I used to bite my nails and cuticles until they almost bled. My father would tease me by quipping, "How about a little salt and pepper on those nails?" or "How about a little ketchup or mustard on those nails?" It looked like I was enjoying a juicy steak. I tried everything—paying for a manicure, applying a bitter substance to coat my nails. Nothing worked until I was about twenty-two years old, and I volunteered to work with a psychologist who was also a hypnotist and was looking for good hypnotic subjects. I was tested and discovered I was a good subject. Dr. Field wanted to perfect his hypnotic technique, and I wanted to learn self-hypnosis and read the hypnosis books he had in his extensive library.

We discovered that most of the time, I wasn't even aware of my biting my nails. The suggestion that finally worked was when the psychologist said to me, "You are a beautiful young lady, and soon you will become engaged. You will want to show your engagement ring to all your friends. Your hands and nails should look as beautiful as your ring. Whenever you become aware of your hand moving toward your mouth, you immediately put your hand down and count to ten. If you still want to bite your nails, then go ahead, but you'll *find you want to have beautiful hands and nails outweighing the need to bite them." We turned these suggestions into self-hypnosis suggestions.*

Suggestion

Whenever I notice my hand moving toward my mouth, I immediately become aware of my hand, put my hand down and count to ten. I have beautiful hands and nails.

I continued with the self-hypnosis suggestion, and when I got engaged the next year, my suggestion changed.

Suggestion

I keep my nails beautifully manicured and enjoy the admiring looks as I show off my engagement ring.

A side note to the above story: My father wanted to know where I was going and what I was doing as I had asked to borrow the car to get to the hospital. I told him I was meeting with a psychologist who would be using hypnosis to help me stop biting my nails. My father insisted my brother go with me to make sure there was no "stuff" going on with the hypnosis. He still had the old-fashioned idea that the hypnotist could "control me," and make me do something against my will. My brother was there to "protect" me. After my brother came with me twice, he assured my father that all was on the up and up, and I was able to go alone.

I was updating my phone at the phone store. As the sales assistant was typing on his computer, I noticed he had beautiful hands with long slender fingers, but the image was marred by the nails that were bitten almost to the quick. I asked him how long he'd been biting his nails, and he answered sheepishly, "Ever since high school." I told him I was a hypnotist and gave him my card. I asked him if he wanted to stop biting his nails. I also asked him if he was ready to stop. He said yes, so I gave him a copy of my self-hypnosis booklet written before this book. I asked him to read the self-hypnosis instructions up to Step 2 and to practice Steps 1 and 2 in the coming week. When I came back to pick up the phone I ordered, I would teach him to formulate his suggestions to stop biting his nails.

Suggestion

I am in control of my hands. Whenever I get the urge to bite my nails, I take three deep breaths, and the urge is replaced by a sense of pride as I have nice nails and hands.

Suggestion

I have manicured nails and hands. The urge to bite them is replaced with admiration as people notice my carefully manicured nails (my beautiful engagement ring), and I feel a sense of pride.

Procrastination

We are all guilty of this bad habit at some point.

One of my clients does accomplish a lot during the day. However, one day she decides she will pay her bills that day. But when she passes the bird cage, she realizes the bird cage needs cleaning, so she cleans it. She makes herself a cup of coffee to drink while she pays her bills and notices she is low on milk, so she goes to the store to get some. While she's going out, she notices she has packages to mail, so she takes these with her to drop off on her way back from the store. By the time she gets back, it is lunchtime, so she makes herself something to eat. She notices that the shelf in the refrigerator needs cleaning, so she takes care of that. By the time she sits down to pay bills, she is so tired she just puts it off until tomorrow. Do you know anyone like that?

75

So how do you avoid getting trapped in a situation like this one? You decide on a day and time when you must pay bills. This date depends on when the bills are due. I break it down to paying bills twice a month, on the 30th of the month, to pay bills due by the 15th of the month before they are due, and again on the 15th of the month to pay bills due by the end of that month.

Give yourself the following suggestion a few days before you must pay bills. As you are giving yourself the suggestion, imagine you are doing the action in the suggestion.

Suggestion

At (10:00 a.m. or whatever you decide) on (date; when you decide), I sit (where; at my desk, at my computer, at the kitchen table) and pay the bills that are due soon, and I (reward; feel a sense of relief, that I accomplished this, good about myself, I enjoy a cup of coffee, tea, hot chocolate, etc.)

What do you procrastinate about? Formulate your suggestion around that. It is most important you give yourself a reward for doing the thing you procrastinate about.

Social Media, Internet, Games, TV

Are you spending too much time during the day on Facebook, Twitter, etc.? Do you surf the internet? Think you watch too much TV? These are habits that can be changed or controlled with self-hypnosis. But remember, you must want to change or control them.

Suggestion

Every morning after breakfast, I post on Facebook (surf the internet, etc) for thirty minutes, and I feel great!

Clutter

I taught my very first self-hypnosis class in a church in 1987. I met the pastor of the church at a conference and hosted a short presentation on the benefits of self-hypnosis. The pastor was an excellent hypnotic subject, and to demonstrate the power of the mind, I suggested that if he believed his arm was a steel bar, he could not bend it. And he could not bend it until I asked him to stop imagining and to relax his arm. He was so impressed with hypnosis he invited me to give a three-week course on self-hypnosis at his church.

One of the members of the church wanted to clear the clutter on her dining room table. She formulated the following suggestion:

Suggestion

Every Tuesday, Thursday, and Saturday at 10:00 a.m., I spend twenty minutes putting items away that are on my dining room table, and because I have a clear table, I invite friends over to dinner and feel proud of myself.

While she was in hypnosis, she imagined a clear dining room table, enjoying dinner with friends sitting around a clear table.

Several years later, my late husband and I joined this church, and several years after that, I attended a bible study at this lady's house. We had coffee and dessert on her clear dining room table!

Do you have a closet, table, garage, attic, desk, kitchen drawer, or cabinet you want to clear? Don't let the job overwhelm you. Pick a corner, shelf, or area you want to work on, formulate your suggestion as above, and then move on to another area.

A client has a pile of magazines she wants to read, but they are cluttering her already overflowing coffee table. You may have the same issue with newspapers, etc.

Suggestion

Every Tuesday and Friday at 10:00 a.m. I go through (insert a number) I received that week (month) and tear out the article(s) I want to read and set them aside to read, and I feel good about keeping a clean coffee table.

You can also make up a suggestion for when you will go through those articles.

Suggestion

Every Sunday at 4:00 p.m., I take out my magazine articles folder and spend (thirty minutes, one hour, etc.) reading the articles and enjoy having this time to myself.

Exercise

A weight-loss client wanted to do aerobic exercise for thirty minutes a day, five days a week. I asked her how often she does aerobic exercise currently. "Oh no," she replied. "I don't do any exercise now." So, I asked her if this was believable. What does she think would happen after ten minutes of aerobics? "Oh, I'll be tired and stop." When that happened, she would believe herself to be a failure, so I helped her make the suggestion more believable.

Suggestion

Every Tuesday, Thursday, and Saturday, I do aerobics for ten minutes, and I become slim and trim.

You need to be specific about what type of exercise you want to do. A suggestion that reads: Every Monday, Tuesday, and

Thursday, I exercise for thirty minutes, and I feel great, is not specific enough. You should pick an exercise you enjoy doing. I, myself, like to line dance. To me, this is an enjoyable activity that I love to do. I start with the Macarena, move on to the Electric Slide, and slow down to the Cha Cha Slide.

Suggestion:

Every (insert days) I walk (jump rope, dance, cycle, etc.) for (insert time) and I keep fit and trim (or other reward).

As you get used to the exercise, you can increase the time and number of days accordingly. Or you can add another exercise.

Sales

Are you achieving your sales goals? How many cold calls do you have to make to get an appointment? How many appointments do you have to have to make a sale? How many sales a month do you have to have to meet a quota? Are there things you should be doing to achieve your sales goals. Do you practice your closing techniques? There are many aspects to sales. In what ways do you need to improve to increase your sales? I'm sure you have books to refer to. Check them and formulate your suggestions accordingly. Some examples follow:

Suggestion

Every day at 10:00 a.m. I spend one hour (whatever you need) making cold calls to get ten appointments a week (for example) to make one sale (insert number), and I meet my sales quota for the month!

Do you have a sales plan? Do you have sales goals?

Suggestion

Every Sunday at 8:00 p.m., I prepare a weekly sales plan and visit twenty-five additional prospects as a result!

How effective is your presentation and your closing techniques? Do you know how to handle objections? Do you practice these techniques until they become second nature? While you are saying the suggestion to yourself, imagine you are making a sales presentation or closing the sale and answering objections.

Suggestion

Every (evening, morning, day of the week) I rehearse (my presentation, closing) to (get the appointment, close the sale), and I feel great and I make more sales, (meet my weekly quote, earn more money.)

Conclusion

What do you need to change, improve, or do differently? Look at the above examples and formulate your suggestion accordingly.

CHAPTER 13

Memory, Test Anxiety, and Concentration

Learning

*I*n 1987, I used self-hypnosis techniques to take my written and oral hypnosis certification exams for the Association to Advance Ethical Hypnosis. There was a lot of material to be learned in the basic and advanced hypnosis courses. I used the sandwich technique outlined below to help with retention and recall to pass the written part of the exam. I used the rehearsal technique when I took the oral part of the certification exam. I imagined myself in front of the certification board, answering their questions and hypnotizing a subject. The in-person test went well. I passed with "flying colors," said Martin Segal, who was then the executive director of the AAEH.

After graduating from high school, I attended Brooklyn College and earned a BA degree with a major in sociology and a minor in education. Using regular study methods, my grades ranged from C+ to B+ with several As in my major. After becoming a certified hypnotist in 1987, I used many of the study techniques outlined in this chapter while attending classes for a yearlong intensive paralegal course in 1994. Each class was worth three credits, and the entire program consisted of ten different classes. I earned eight

As and two Bs with an overall grade point average of 3.8. This was a big improvement over my college grades.

In this chapter, we will deviate from the self-hypnosis formula to learn the sandwich method. I will also give you suggestions to help you develop a better memory.

Hypnosis works!

The human mind can recall virtually any information that it desires to remember. The most important word in the process is "desire." The human mind is of such size that it could not be filled in a total lifetime. It can remember everything it has ever heard, read, or experienced. Hypnosis can be a highly effective procedure for stimulating the learning process—increasing motivation, establishing beneficial study habits, boosting confidence, reducing study and examination tensions, and accessing memory. Hypnosis can also be applied to goal setting and achievement. Students of all ages can acquire study habits that will provide benefits for a lifetime. Adults and working people in all occupations can gain the motivation to undertake continuing educational studies, adding to existing knowledge/skills or developing new fields of interest for income generation, recreation, or personal satisfaction. Hypnosis can help a person define their purpose and direction. Attitudes can be changed, poor habit patterns can be overcome, enthusiasm can be developed, and self-respect and self-esteem can be increased.

The amount of information necessary to be a knowledgeable individual is increasing at a rapid rate. For some individuals, the amount of data to learn is overwhelming. They require a new approach to learning. Hypnosis has proven to be effective in enhancing standard learning techniques. Through hypnosis, individuals are taught to take control of their learning habits. Hypnosis is used to strengthen motivation, facilitate study habits, improve concentration, enhance recall, and alleviate exam jitters. Learning cannot take place without motivation! A negative attitude toward studying is effectively reduced by improving motivation through hypnosis. Most people do not have the ability to concentrate; they have an aversion to studying.

Hypnosis can increase a person's attention span and make studying more rewarding and less of a chore. Hypnosis assists the person in absorbing new material rapidly and easily recalling it. Because the hypnotist cannot be readily available to the individual for each study session, the individual learns self-hypnosis. The capabilities lie within the individual. Hypnosis and self-hypnosis enable the person to take advantage of their abilities. With proper hypnotic conditioning, mental faculties are enormously enhanced, and self-hypnosis helps reinforce these mental faculties.

Study Habits

External conditions can affect study habits. Most important is the physical location of the study area. This location should be used whenever one studies. A learner who has a specific location in an area where external distractions are eliminated, including but not limited to TV, CD/MP3 player, cell phone, radio, people traffic, will learn much more effectively. Concentration is essential, and the learner should leave the designated area when concentration becomes difficult. In any case, a ten-minute break every thirty to forty-five minutes will improve learning. Hypnosis can be used to focus concentration and block out external distractions.

Memory

The subconscious mind remembers everything that has happened and can recall it on request, whether it is a memory of a past event, the location of a misplaced item, material to be studied or names, addresses, telephone numbers, or other information that is needed at a specific time or for a specific purpose.

There are three types of memory: sensory memory dealing with functions like seeing, smelling, feeling, hearing, and tasting; motor skill memory involving remembering how to perform physical activities like riding a bicycle, driving a car, swimming, dancing, etc., and the most vital one to learning is memory of words, ideas, and concepts. This is the least retentive type of memory and perhaps the most complex.

The key first step is the organization of the meaningful material to be learned into a logical pattern, emphasizing the broadest concept, the theme, then narrowing the focus to appropriate specifics.

To remember material, you first must perceive it, see it, hear it, or become aware of it through one of your senses. Then you need to retain it in your short-term memory long enough to store it in some organized, classified way in your long-term memory. And finally, you must be able to find it so that you can recall it on demand.

What goes into your memory? Why do some memories last and others fade? Emotions play a strong role in memory. I'm sure many of us can recall exactly where we were and what we were doing the moment we heard about the planes crashing into the Twin Towers on September 11, 2001. On TV, I witnessed the second plane crashing into the second tower and the subsequent collapse of both towers. I was at work, and our boss told us to go into his office and turn on the TV! This was an emotional moment. Think back to other strong memories. Chances are a strong emotion was linked to many of them. But we usually don't remember insignificant details such as the direction Lincoln faces on the penny. Okay, you can take one out and check. I will wait. That's right. Lincoln faces right! Naturally, our personal experiences and interests define the level of significance we attribute to events and information and, therefore, to how memorable these events and material will be for us.

People complain about having a poor memory. They say, "I forgot" or "I can't remember." Aside from the physiological or psychological reasons we forget, say, a dentist's appointment, the important point is that you cannot forget what you have not learned in the first place. In other words, forgetting is measured by the inability to remember after learning has taken place. A person who complains about his inability to remember usually failed to properly learn the material in the first place.

Time Management

Time management, or lack thereof, can create an unnecessary drain on energy and emotions and adversely affect the learning process. The answer lies in the organization of the material to be studied. You should review all the material you need to learn and break the material to be studied into small, easily accomplishable segments of thirty to forty-five minutes each. For example, you have a month to learn ten chapters in a textbook. Thirty days translates into a chapter every ten days. Four weeks translates into two and a half chapters per week. You can further break it down into so many pages a day. Then decide on the number of pages you will study per day. Another parameter to consider is how many days a week you want to study. Break it down into manageable chunks of time of thirty to forty-five minutes, decide on the time of day you will study and the day(s) of the week you will study, and you have a plan.

Reward

A powerful element in learning is self-reward. Recognition of personal achievement, self-congratulation, and self-appreciation are expressed through reward. Advance determination of self-reward plans creates anticipation, motivation, and personal desire. Small rewards at various levels of progress tend to maintain excitement and stimulus, especially where a list of anticipated rewards is maintained with a completion timetable. Some suggested rewards: read a book or magazine, spend time on Facebook or other social media, watch a movie, listen to an MP3, take a long shower or a bubble bath.

Self-Esteem

Self-esteem, so important in motivation, may be invisible, but it is a powerful force. When it obstructs learning, the learner is a prime candidate for hypnosis. The learner, through self-hypnosis, can acquire the ability to relax at will, experience feelings of confidence, or can use a cue to bring awareness of control, motivation for success, or the ability to defuse a fearful situation.

Identify the Problem

To improve your learning ability, you must first identify the difficulty. Most people have problems with one or more of the following:

1. Impression or Registration

When a person sits down to study, the material that he must learn has to be impressed upon his mind. If he's concentrating on what he's studying, the material makes a deep impression and is therefore registered. However, if the person has difficulty concentrating due to distractions from the environment, that is, sounds of children, traffic noises, television or radio playing, etc., the material makes a weak impression and is incompletely or imperfectly impressed.

Suggestion

Whenever I study, I block out all distractions and focus on the material in front of me.

2. Retention

Once something is registered, it is learned, and then it is retained. If not immediately or frequently recalled, that which has been learned is "archived" in the brain for recall at a future time. There is evidence that once something is learned, it's never forgotten. However, it's also true that new material, not immediately recalled, is archived, and possibly superimposed upon older archived material. This sometimes modifies or combines the individual's information. The span of retention is, therefore, an important factor in preventing two or more individual bits of information from being altered. This retention span differs with the importance of the information and the requirements of the individual.

Suggestion

I easily retain all that I have studied and pass the test with flying colors.

3. Recall and Remembering

Some people, for a variety of reasons, are unable to easily recall material they have learned. They could experience psychological blocks such as nervousness. These blocks affect the recall of newly learned as well as archived information. Forgetting is simply the inability to easily remember.

Suggestion

I can easily recall and remember all that I have studied, and I pass the test with flying colors.

Exam Preparation

For exam preparation, I recommend several combined techniques. In addition to using self-hypnosis to study the material, you also give yourself several suggestions during your review of the material the night before the exam. At the end of the review session, you give yourself the following suggestions:

During the examination (test, quiz), whatever I have learned flows freely and easily through my mind. Whatever I have learned is always available in my memory. During the examination, I remain calm, at ease, and composed. My mind works very smoothly.

You must understand that hypnosis is not "magic"! You **must study** the material before the test, but hypnosis will make studying and remembering easier. As the day of the exam nears, you can rehearse taking the exam while in hypnosis. Put yourself into hypnosis and imagine yourself in the exam room, taking the exam paper, reading over all the questions. You might even make up some questions and see and feel yourself easily answering the questions. Feel the answers flow from your mind into your writing hand as you see and feel yourself writing the answers. If it is an oral exam, see yourself in the room and hear the questions being asked and hear yourself and imagine yourself giving the appropriate answers to the questions.

If you are studying for a mid-term, final, or a special exam (CPA, GRE, MCAT, etc.) that has a deadline, prepare, and commit a study plan to paper and incorporate the plan in your daily self-hypnosis suggestions to complete the required study material. For example: If you have an exam scheduled for the end of June and there are five months in which to cover the material consisting of twenty-five chapters or lessons, that breaks down to five chapters or lessons a month or one and one-quarter lessons a week or so many numbers of pages a day etc.

Suggestion for Studying

For one hour (insert time) every day (or every other day, or specify the days), I can easily find the time to study one lesson (chapters, pages) each week (or insert the day) and can easily retain and recall all the material studied and I ace the test.

Suggestion for Rehearsing Taking an Exam

On (day of exam) when I take the (type of exam) exam, all the material that I studied easily flows into my mind and I (insert reward such as ace the exam, graduate, obtain my MBA, become a CPA, get my (type) license).

The technique to use while studying is called the "Sandwich Method" and is different than the self-hypnosis technique described in this book. I've included it here to help you with your studying. You can use it nightly or use it to motivate you to stick to a certain study schedule. You can use it to rehearse taking an exam. You may also use this method to improve self-esteem and increase your self-confidence or for general memory improvement.

The Sandwich Method

Once the area(s) of difficulty have been identified, suggestions can be formulated and then given under hypnosis to change the individual's learning techniques. Suggestions must be positive, employing words and phrases that express the desired goal. The secret of studying is in the ability to focus concentration until the material is learned. This requires the ability to impress or register the information and retain it.

The key to the ability to learn is in effective studying. Mr. Harry Arons describes in his book *The New Master Course in Hypnotism,* the sandwich technique in which hypnosis is effectively used in learning. Arons calls this the sandwich technique because the person puts himself in hypnosis for the suggestions and then brings himself out of hypnosis to study. He then puts himself back in hypnosis for suggestions to retain the material just studied. The studying is "sandwiched" between the self-hypnosis. This method is ideal for problem-solving, studying, and reading. You give yourself the suggestion before studying.

Suggestion

Whenever I need to, I will retain and easily recall studied material.

Suggestion

My concentration gets better and better, and my mind is always pinpointed on what I am studying, reading, or focusing on.

This method is also excellent for improving concentration and for motivation, e.g., motivating yourself to study for a required period. This is also an effective method to minimize distractions during study time. Determine where, when, how, and under what conditions you study best, then enhance the environment hypnotically.

Suggestions

Whenever I sit down to study, I am so completely absorbed in my studying that all outside distractions fade away, and I can completely concentrate on the material at hand.

You then study for the required period. There is a theory that people recall better when studying is done in short thirty to forty-five-minute chunks. After studying, you again put yourself in hypnosis and give yourself suggestion(s).

Suggestion

All the material that I have just learned is permanently retained. Whatever I have learned is easily recalled.

You then emerge from hypnosis and take a ten-minute break. Do whatever you want during this break. Get a drink of water, walk around the block, etc. You are then ready for your next thirty to forty-five-minute segment of study. Again, sit down in your study place and put yourself into hypnosis. Repeat the same suggestion you did before or choose another, depending on your area of difficulty as described previously. Most people, after applying these suggestions, report improved memory, higher levels of concentration, less general tension, and improved sleep as a benefit of self-hypnosis.

CHAPTER 14

Performance Enhancement

Sports

Many athletes have used hypnosis and hypnotic techniques to enhance their performance. The following is just a small sampling of reported athletes and teams who have used hypnosis, guided imagery, or visualization.

Tiger Woods' father wanted his boy to excel at golf, so when Tiger was a young teen, his father contacted a friend and psychologist he met in the military to hypnotize Tiger to play better golf. Tiger learned to hypnotize himself to be "in the zone" and fully concentrate on the game. Tiger would use the power of self-hypnosis to visualize every swing and stroke in his mind before he executed the stroke or putt. He "saw" in his mind exactly where he wanted the ball to go. He also used self-hypnosis to focus totally on the game, and he was able to eliminate the distractions of the crowds.

You should:

- Remain positive on each shot attempt.

- Before you play the course, identify the trouble spots of each hole before deciding on the proper distance and trajectory point needed to hit the green.
- Remember the suggestions you gave yourself before your shot.
- Reduce anxiety by focusing on the process instead of the results.
- Change your mindset from defensive to offensive thinking.

Many athletes use the power of visualization to enhance their performance. I remember watching the twin brothers Phil and Steve Mahre during the 1984 Olympics. While they were still in the chute, just before their downhill run, a look of total concentration was on their faces. They were visualizing the course as they practiced every turn in their minds. Steve won the silver medal in slalom.

Figure skating coaches use hypnosis not only to have their skaters rehearse their performance but to cancel a bad rehearsal or performance from their minds. The skaters were conditioned to use hypnosis and self-hypnosis. Some figure skaters who have used hypnosis and hypnotic techniques to improve their skating, overcome performance anxiety, and concentrate and memorize their performance are Brian Orser, Dorothy Hamill, and Kristi Yamaguchi, to name a few. Brian, who is now a coach, teaches hypnotic techniques to his students.

If you are a figure skater, you know skating requires athletic agility and stamina. Since the ice responds directly to your emotions and ability, it also requires that you remain calm while performing in front of a crowd. Add the extremely competitive nature of professional skating, and it can sometimes be too much to handle.

Competitive figure skating requires the skater to have complete mental confidence in themselves and their abilities. Self-hypnosis gives you the ability to focus and concentrate. You know how your body must move to execute the spins and jumps. Visualize yourself performing those routines in front of a crowd. Self-hypnosis can also help you remember your routines and help you remain calm.

When you are giving yourself the suggestion during your self-hypnosis session, you visualize yourself doing what you are suggesting.

Suggestion

When I (hear the music, skate onto the ice), I become calm, relaxed, and focused. I easily remember the moves and skate my routine perfectly.

When the Russian pair skater fell on the ice, their coach called to them to come to the rail. She immediately passed her hand in front of the eyes of the one who fell and quietly said, "Cancel." While you should always make your suggestions positive, in this instance, the coach is canceling the fall, so the skater doesn't dwell on it.

Suggestion

When I make a mistake, I immediately say "cancel" to myself, and I do better in future skates.

During the 1984 Olympics, *TIME* magazine reported that on the night before the finals in women's gymnastics, famous athlete Mary Lou Retton, then age sixteen, would mentally rehearse her routines before going to sleep, visualizing herself performing all her routines perfectly. The result, of course, was a performance of perfection, a score of a perfect 10, and she received the gold medal.

Suggestion

As I fall asleep, I visualize my performance (whatever the sport) executed perfectly, and I score high marks.

Most of you may not know about Rod Carew who played baseball from 1967 to 1985. After he suffered an injury, he was still experiencing pain and doubted his abilities to play baseball. He began to see a hypnotist, who helped him overcome his disabilities and self-doubt and ended his career with a batting average close to .400 and went on to win the AL Most Valuable Player Award.

There were other players who also used hypnosis and self-hypnosis during their careers to help them relax and focus during games: Nolan Ryan, George Brett, Maury Wills, Don Sutton, and Mark McGwire, to name a few.

One of my clients wanted to play better golf. She told me that whenever she approached the "water hole," she would reach for her "water ball." If you play golf, you know the one. It's the ball you can afford to lose in the water! Do you know what you're doing? You're giving yourself a negative suggestion! You approach the water and assume you're going to lose the ball, and so you do hit that ball into the water.

Suggestion

Whenever I approach the water hole (sand trap, tree, bush, or other obstacle), I focus on where I want that ball to go

and hit the ball to land where I want it to land and feel great (confident, self-assured, etc.).

Suggestion:

Whenever I practice my (fill in what you need to improve; putting, long shots, double axels, ice dancing routines, sit spins, etc.) for (fill in the time you are willing to spend, i.e., fifteen minutes) every (morning, day, Monday, Wednesday, and Friday, etc.) and I (insert reward; feel great, take two strokes off my score, hear the applause of my audience, etc.).

Creativity

Scott Adams used hypnotic suggestion to enhance his career. He would tell himself over and over he would create a number one comic strip and be successful. He was the creator of the comic strip *Dilbert* which became very popular.

Do you paint, write, or play a musical instrument? What is your goal? I used self-hypnosis to stick to a schedule to write this book.

Suggestion

Whenever I (write, paint, draw, or fill in what you need to do) for (fill in the time you are willing to spend, i.e., fifteen minutes) on (day, every morning, Monday, Wednesday, and Friday, etc.), I (insert reward; feel great, create a . . . drawing, picture, article, book, etc.).

Performance Anxiety

I loaned a friend a book about hypnosis. He had anxiety about playing the piano in front of an audience during a recital arranged by his piano teacher. He played flawlessly when he was alone or in front of his wife but froze when in front of others. After reading that hypnosis could help with this, he came to me to teach him self-hypnosis. I taught him to visualize himself playing at the recital and performing perfectly. He would think about how he would feel after playing, how proud he was, and how the audience applauded him. He would visualize the performance going great.

Suggestion

Whenever I play in front of an audience, I am calm, relaxed, and in control. I hear the applause of the crowd, and I feel great.

Suggestion

Before I perform, I take three deep breaths, and I feel calm, relaxed, and in control.

My friend programmed in each of these suggestions using one a day for two weeks during his three-minute self-hypnosis sessions. The week before the performance, he used the last one:

Suggestion

Whenever I take three deep breaths, I feel calm, relaxed, and in control.

Now when he performs, all he needs to do before the performance is to take three deep breaths, and he IS calm, relaxed, and in control.

A client was asked to give a speech at a memorial service. She wasn't comfortable speaking in public. I taught her self-hypnosis for performance

97

Joann Abrahamsen

anxiety. She wrote out her speech, put herself into hypnosis, and imagined herself in front of the people giving the eulogy. She had previously programmed herself with the suggestion below, so when she gave the eulogy, she was relaxed and delivered the eulogy perfectly.

Suggestion

Whenever I take three deep breaths, I feel calm, relaxed, and in control.

Do you get nervous speaking in public? Fear of speaking in public is the most common fear, ahead of fear of death, fear of spiders, and fear of heights. The underlying fear is incurring judgment or negative evaluations by others. The first thing you must realize is many people fear speaking in public, even famous people like Abraham Lincoln, Margaret Sanger, and Winston Churchill. Becoming a good speaker cannot happen overnight. Identify the problem. Reframe the butterflies in your stomach to excitement. You must prepare.

Knowing what you're going to say is the first step. Next, begin on a high note. Tell a story that relates to the subject. Begin with a joke if you're comfortable. Then focus on your audience. Craft your speech keeping the audience's goals in mind. Make eye contact. You don't have to look at everyone—just focus on one individual at a time. Let your gaze wander from left to right. Believe in what you're saying. Keep in mind that the audience generally wants you to succeed. Practice in front of a mirror, your spouse, and your friends. Join Toastmasters or a similar group where you must make presentations. Practice, practice, practice.

Circle of Excellence

Do you remember the lemon experiment we did previously? I asked you to imagine that you were holding a lemon in your hand. Look at it, describe it, cut it open. Look at the juicy, cut lemon. Now squeeze the lemon and feel the juice drop into your hand. Now take a bite of the lemon. Are you salivating? If you are, great. If you are not, that's okay too, as the following technique works if you use that wonderful imagination of yours.

Using a technique called the circle of excellence, we're going to create an "as if" resource state. A resource state refers to any state of mind where a person has positive, helpful emotions and strategies available to them and is operating from them behaviorally. Obviously, the state implies a successful outcome. What state do you want to create? Self-confidence? How do you want to feel?

Circle of Excellence Script

1. Go Back in the Moment and Relive the Experience

Stand up and go back to a time when you felt extremely confident. You can use any positive emotion, but for the purpose of this exercise, I use confidence.

Relive that moment; see what you saw, listen to what you heard, and feel what you felt. If it is related to food, you can add taste and smell too. This will amplify the effect.

2. Make a Spot (Circle of Excellence)

Imagine you draw a circle on the floor. Draw it as big as you can stand in it comfortably.

Put whatever color you want inside the circle, associate it with sound, if any, relive the feeling of confidence, and direct it into the circle.

If you need to, add more colors, clarify the sound, and increase the feeling(s) as much as possible.

3. When the Experience Reaches Its Peak, Step into the Circle

Relive the moment. Feel the feeling going through your body and outside your body. This sensation makes you feel even more confident.

4. Think of a Time in the Future

Notice where you need this feeling of confidence in the future.

Imagine a situation where you may require these positive emotions. See yourself dealing with that situation with this new positive emotion.

You can now deal with these situations better.

5. Repeat the Process

Maybe you want to use the same emotion, say confidence, but at a different time than you did before. If you can't think of another situation, think of a person you admire that had the trait you desire. How would that person act, feel, etc.?

Take a few deep breaths and feel that positive emotion inside you performing in that circle.

Now repeat the process as many times as possible to strengthen the circle. I anchor this feeling by touching my thumb and forefinger together on my dominant hand as if making an OK sign. See the explanation of anchoring below.

6. Step Out of the Circle

. . . taking those positive feelings and emotions with you.

7. Test It

Step into the circle again and feel those positive feelings and emotions flowing through you.

8. Step Out of the Circle

. . . taking those positive feelings and emotions with you.

9. Take the Circle

Imagine you can fold the circle into a tiny, small pack and keep it in your pocket, purse, or wallet. These positive emotions are now always available to you just in your pocket, purse, or wallet. You can just pull out these emotions from your pocket, put them in front of your eyes, and feel those positive feelings again.

The circle can also work well along with anchoring. Anchoring refers to the process of associating an internal response or a positive feeling or emotion (like confidence) with some external or internal trigger so that the response may be quickly, and sometimes covertly, accessed. You can touch your thumb and forefinger together, tap your foot, and/or just say a word. I would use "confidence" or "excellence."

This circle of excellence script can be altered as per your need. You can also just visualize the circle in your mind as you perform the steps. I have just shared what has worked for me. I use this circle of excellence when I do a presentation. If you read my chapter on memory and learning, I used a version of this before I took my hypnosis certification exam.

In this chapter, we have viewed different aspects of performance and have suggested various aspects. Only you know which area(s) you want to improve. I'm sure you have books that will point you in the right direction. You may also have instructors or coaches who work with you to improve whatever activity you're engaged in. Many people hire life coaches to help them improve their life. I do online life coaching also. Check out my website www.joannabrahamsen.com and make a free consultation appointment to see if I can help you achieve your goals.

CHAPTER 15

Medical Applications

Pain Management

From Roy Hunter's Foreword;

"After suffering a permanent back injury in the early 1980s, I discovered the benefits of hypnosis and self-hypnosis for taming chronic pain enough to live a normal life; [and in 1983, I decided to become a hypnotherapist.]"

The use of hypnosis and self-hypnosis for controlling and managing pain is well documented in many books, articles, and journals. Those patients who received self-hypnosis instruction had much less pain and anxiety than those without instruction.

I am using the word "pain" here, so we know what we're talking about. However, the word itself has a negative connotation. When using hypnosis to reduce or minimize pain, I like to use the word "discomfort" instead.

While self-hypnosis can be used to reduce or minimize pain, you must make sure the cause of the pain has been diagnosed and treated. Pain is a signal that there's something wrong with the body. If you get rid of the pain from a broken ankle and continue to walk on it, you will do damage to your ankle. If you get rid of a constant headache, you may be masking a tumor. So, before you use hypnosis for pain, use common sense and see a doctor first. However, if you're using hypnosis to reduce or minimize chronic pain, make sure you've been diagnosed with a chronic condition before you reduce or eliminate the pain.

When you are in hypnosis, you are usually relaxed. Relaxation alone can minimize pain because when we relax, fewer pain impulses go from the site of the pain to the brain, causing an analgesic effect.

If you are tense, the pain impulses increase, causing you to feel the pain more. Hypnosis can cause profound relaxation, so take advantage of this when working with yourself. Relaxation will change the your perception of pain.

Feeling pain is subjective. Can you remember a time when you were out playing with your friends, and you scraped your knee? You ignored the pain and continued to play. It was only when you went inside, and your mother noticed your scraped knee that you felt the pain and maybe cried a little for sympathy.

Little Johnny fell while playing outside and scraped his knee. He went running to his mother, crying. "Aw," said his mom. "Let me kiss the boo-boo and make it better." Was Little Johnny's mom using hypnosis? Yes, she was. Little Johnny believed his mother's kiss would make the boo-boo feel better. And it did!

Many athletes are injured while playing competitive sports. Because their attention is placed elsewhere, they don't feel any pain from their injuries until the game is over. Whatever you pay attention to increases. If you give your pain attention, it will increase. If you can detach from it and pay it less attention, it will decrease. A lot can be said about the adage, "To get rid of a headache, hit your toe with a hammer." Don't worry. I'm not going to suggest you do that. What I am going to suggest is that you learn a technique called "the control room." Using this technique, you can reduce or even eliminate pain.

To do this technique, you need to be in a light state of hypnosis. To get yourself to this state quickly, you are first going to say the following suggestion to yourself and practice this suggestion a few times.

Suggestion

Whenever I sit in a comfortable chair and take three deep breaths (count backward from 5 to 1), I put my hands on my lap (or whatever signal you give yourself). I immediately close my eyes and enter a hypnotic state.

Remember, I stated earlier that once you learn self-hypnosis, you can enter the hypnotic state anytime you wish. Whenever I want to enter the hypnotic state, I put my thumb and forefingers of both hands together in an OK sign, take three deep breaths, count backward from 3 to 1, and I'm there.

While you are in hypnosis, you now use the power of your imagination. Imagine you are in a room with lots of dials, levers, and controls of every kind. You may imagine you are in a cockpit as the pilot of an airplane. I imagine myself sitting at the controls of a spaceship. If nothing comes to mind, look on the internet for "control room with levers and dials." The key is to have access to controls, dials, and levers with numbers indicated on them from 9 down to 0.

Imagine this control panel gives you access to all systems in the body. Notice what controls apply to the part of your body that is in pain. Notice at what level your discomfort is at this point. Give it a number from 9 being the greatest lever of discomfort to 0 being no discomfort. Now imagine yourself reaching out with your hand and turning down the dial that controls your pain level in that part of the body. As you turn down the dial, notice how you feel. Give it a number. Repeat the process until you are at a level where you are more comfortable.

Even as I sit here typing this book, I'm going to pause for a few moments and use this technique on my right leg as I have stenosis in my lower spine, which sometimes causes me lower back pain or pain in my leg if I sit too long. This situation is not good for a writer as I need to sit at my computer and type, and I wanted to finish this book you are holding. I pause. I allow myself to enter hypnosis. I do the technique. This time, I imagine I'm the captain of the starship USS Enterprise, and I can manage all the controls, levers, and dials from the captain's chair. That's better. I reduced the level of discomfort from 6 down to 2. I continue to type, feeling better. If I took the time to pause again, I could bring the number down to 0, but I wanted to finish this part of the book.

I have rolling veins. I use the following suggestion during my self-hypnosis session several times before going to the doctor:

Suggestion

Whenever I need to have my blood drawn, I relax my arm and allow the coolness of the alcohol to numb my skin as if my arm (hand) was dipped into a bucket of ice water (or a handful of snow or an ice cube was rubbed on the spot.) My blood is drawn successfully.

Remember to stay relaxed. While you may feel some discomfort, it will be a lot less than if you did nothing.

My neighbor needed surgery. I had hypnotized her prior for weight loss, and she knew that hypnosis could help her stay relaxed and recover faster before going into surgery. I went to the hospital at 6:00 the morning of her surgery. She had gotten permission from the doctors for me to hypnotize her before they did the operation. I hypnotized her and gave her suggestions for being calm and relaxed. I told her to trust the surgeon. She would only hear positive comments while under anesthesia. She would heal quickly. They rolled her out of the prep room singing.

In 2020, I was diagnosed with breast cancer. I had a partial mastectomy to remove the tumor. My treatment involved several months of chemotherapy followed by two months of radiation. Using self-hypnosis, I gave myself suggestions for numbness when the needle for chemo had to be inserted and for the blood drawn, just like the suggestions above. I used self-hypnosis to remain still during all the MRIs and radiation treatments. Remember I said earlier that I also used humor to help me through the treatments? I always asked for 60s music to be played during the radiation treatment. When I was on the table, and a dance tune played like "Do You Love Me?" or "Twist and Shout," I joked and cried out, "Not fair. I want to jump off the table and dance and I can't."

Suggestion

Whenever I need to remain still like during an MRI or radiation treatment, I remain calm and still and can stay in that position for as long as the hospital staff asks me to.

My husband Robert, who is also a hypnotist, gave me hypnotic suggestions at home between chemo treatments, to reduce the effects of the treatment. I cannot repeat the suggestions here as a qualified hypnotist needs to apply the suggestions with an appropriate referral from a doctor. Contact me if you would want to pursue this. One of my future books will be about my cancer journey. See the pages at the beginning of this book to get on my mailing list to be notified about my future books.

Dental

I was just learning about hypnosis when my dentist told me I needed gum surgery to save my teeth. He had to cut the gums so the teeth would remain attached to the bone. I needed surgery on my whole mouth. We did a quadrant—one quarter—at a time. I discovered I could hypnotize myself not to feel any pain. I could feel touch but no pain. I asked the dentist if I could have one of the surgeries without Novocain. "Oh no," he exclaimed! "I wouldn't be comfortable operating on you without you being anesthetized."

I assured him I could do it. To convince him of the power of hypnosis, I offered to hypnotize him to experience hypnosis for himself. So, one evening after he saw his last patient, I had him recline in the dental chair and hypnotized him. I gave him the suggestion that his eyelids were so relaxed that he couldn't open them no matter how hard he tried. He was very surprised to find he couldn't open his eyes until I told him he could. He accepted the suggestion that his eyes couldn't open, and they didn't. This blew his mind. He said that the final surgery was on a part of my mouth that didn't require much cutting, so I could use self-hypnosis then. In preparation for the surgery, I gave myself the following self-hypnosis suggestion.

Suggestion

As long as I focus on the overhead light, feel my hands on the arms of the chair, and hear the water in the basin, I would remain comfortable. I may feel some pressure, tugging, and pulling, but I remain relaxed and comfortable.

I went through the surgery without any pain, but I did feel pressure, pulling, and tugging. I only wanted to do this to prove to myself that I could, but I wouldn't recommend it. I always take Novocain. I do use self-hypnosis, however, to suggest that all I feel is a little pressure when getting the Novocain injection. I had a dentist who, just before he gave me the Novocain injection, used to take my cheek, and slightly pinch and wiggle it as he gave me the shot. So, while the brain is wondering "what's he doing," the conscious mind is distracted, and that distraction lessened the feel of the injection.

In my opinion, it's easier to see a qualified hypnotist to help you with your pain management. They have experience and can help you manage your pain, especially chronic pain, easier than if you just relied on self-hypnosis alone.

Go to my website for a free consultation:
www.joannabrahamsen.com

CHAPTER 16

You Can Change Your Life

Hypnosis is not magic, but it IS magical. In this book, I have given you the tools to change your life and achieve your goals. It's up to you to take that first step and identify the goal(s) you want to achieve. Learn the three steps for self-hypnosis, formulate your suggestions, and then apply self-hypnosis. There are only two reasons self-hypnosis doesn't work: maybe you didn't formulate the suggestion correctly. Go back and review the "How to Formulate Suggestions" chapter. But the main reason self-hypnosis doesn't work is maybe you didn't want to make the change in the first place. In that case, pick another goal for the change you want to make.

While one book cannot possibly contain information for all applications of hypnosis, I have included the most common issues people use self-hypnosis for.

You have the power and control over your life. Learning any new technique takes time and practice. Remember when you learned something new? Perhaps it was learning to drive a car or using a computer. You had to practice the technique until you could do it without any conscious thought. Once you learn self-hypnosis, you have this tool for life to use at will for whatever change you want to make.

For more ideas regarding suggestions, you should refer to other books that deal with your issue(s), such as weight loss, exercise, cooking and eating healthy food, stopping smoking, stress, memory, sales, sports enhancement, peak performance, procrastination, and so on. The internet is a good source also. Follow the steps of self-hypnosis and formulate your suggestions following the guidelines.

Congratulations on finishing this book. You know what changes you need to make to achieve your goals and to be successful in all your future endeavors. All it takes are three steps and three minutes to change your life!

Good luck!

APPENDIX A

Self-Hypnosis Worksheet

Overall goal I wish to achieve.

_____

By when _____

Using the guidelines in this book, write one of your suggestions
here.

_____

_____

_____

_____

_____

_____

_____

Reread the guidelines and rewrite here.

_____

_____

_____

_____

_____

APPENDIX B

A Brief History of Hypnosis

The first mention of a possible application of hypnosis is in the Bible; "And the Lord God caused a deep sleep to fall upon Adam, and he slept; and He took one of his ribs..."— Genesis 2:21–22 (KJV)

The Egyptians and the ancient Greeks practiced a trance-like state of sleep in which they believed they would be healed or cured of ailments. The trance was believed to be of a divine nature and of spiritual origin. It was thought to be effective in exorcising evil spirits and intensifying good spirits. Early writings record many magi, fakirs, priests, priestesses, medicine men, and shamans practicing the techniques of laying on their hands and healing with their spoken words.

Dr. Franz Anton Mesmer was a German physician working in Austria who, circa 1776, began to scientifically investigate the trance-like state of sleep. Mesmer believed that the universe exerted a mysterious force upon all life that acted as a magnet and that disease was caused by an unequal distribution of this force over the human body. Mesmer believed that he could regulate the force by passing his hands over the body and curing the individual, giving us the terms "mesmerize" and "mesmerism." Benjamin Franklin and a team of investigators were appointed by the French government to investigate. They declared Mesmer a fraud and stated there was more to warrant further investigation, mentioning "imagination" as a possible factor.

Émile Coué studied pharmacy in Paris and later studied hypnosis at the Nancy School. As a pharmacist, Coué noticed that giving waking suggestions along with medication brought about cures, while medication alone was often ineffective. He developed his own ideas about suggestion and coined the popular phrase: "Every day, in every way, I am getting better and better."

Dr. James Braid coined the word "hypnosis," which is a Greek word meaning "sleep." Dr. Braid named it as such because it appeared to him that the person was sleeping. Further experiments proved that the person was "awake" in that he was able to hear and was aware of all that was around him but very relaxed and focused on the words of the hypnotist. Braid later wanted to change the term to "monoideism," but it was too late. The word "hypnosis" stuck.

Dr. James Esdaile, a surgeon in India, used hypnosis for anesthesia and performed many surgeries, including amputations. Today, there are many medical applications for hypnosis.

Dr. Milton Erickson was an American psychiatrist who specialized in medical hypnosis and family therapy. He was considered the father of modern hypnosis and used stories to help people change. The Ericksonian approach departs from traditional hypnosis in a variety of ways. His approach stressed the importance of the interactive therapeutic relationship and purposeful engagement of the inner resources and experiential life of the subject.

APPENDIX C

How I Became Interested in Hypnosis

The ad on the back of a superhero comic book read, "*The Key to Hypnotism*, only $1.00." The book promised to teach you how to hypnotize anyone. As a precocious twelve-year-old, I was intrigued by all things mystical. I put a one-dollar bill in an envelope, addressed it, stamped it, and anxiously awaited my book. The book arrived in about three weeks.

I skipped over the brief history of hypnosis and went directly to the chapter on "How to Hypnotize." I read the easiest way to hypnotize someone was to have them stare at a fixation point. The easiest one to make consisted of a black button about two inches in diameter with a white dot in the center. Then you asked the subject to stare at the white dot while holding it slightly above their eyes and proceeded with the hypnotic patter. I learned the hypnotic patter was what you said to the subject to get them to go into hypnosis.

I called out to my mother and asked her if she would participate in an experiment for a school science project. As I was a smart student, she trusted me completely. I had her sit down in a comfortable chair and held the button in front of her, slightly above her eyes. I know she was hypnotized because when I gently lifted her eyelids, she was looking up. The book said this was one of the signs. Now that I had her hypnotized, I wondered how to bring her out of hypnosis. I flipped to the back of the book, and it said just to count from 1 to 5 and ask her to open her eyes.

But I was really hooked when, at eighteen, I saw a stage show at a Greenwich Village coffee house. "Come and see The Great Gardino" was the poster slogan. He gave an excellent explanation of hypnosis and then hypnotized his assistant. He called for volunteers. I volunteered and discovered I was a somnambule—a deep hypnotic subject. He gave me the suggestion to count from 1 to 10, skipping the number 7. I counted 1, 2, 3, 4, 5, 6, 8, 9, 10. I read everything I could and bought many books published by Melvin Powers in the countless bookstores along Fifth Avenue in Manhattan.

Fast forward to college when I volunteered to be an experimental subject for a psychologist in a hospital. He needed a deep hypnotic subject to develop his hypnotic techniques, and he would teach me self-hypnosis. I had access to all his hypnosis books. We worked together for a year, and he got to practice and perfect his hypnotic techniques while I learned self-hypnosis and used it to study and take tests.

In the fall of 1986, I took a three-hour class at The Learning Annex entitled "Become a Certified Hypnotist—a Lucrative New Income Opportunity." The class was taught by Richard Harte at a high school in Manhattan. I enjoyed the class and was very interested in learning more. I was in Richard's very first basic hypnosis class. I then took his advanced class and then his five-month internship. I was hooked! I took as many classes in hypnosis as I could find. I bought VHS tapes with training by Milton Erickson, Jerry Kein, and Jerry Valley. I bought Dave Elman's training on cassette from Jerry Kein. My hypnosis library grew by leaps and bounds. When a colleague told me about a hypnosis conference that was being held in Manhattan in 1989, I registered immediately. That was my first NGH conference, and since then, I have attended every NGH convention held since 1989 except one. I began to speak at conferences, and in 1990 I started to self-publish booklets about hypnosis.

I had a full-time job working in an insurance agency, so my practice was part-time at evenings and weekends. Currently, I still practice part-time. I began seeing "clients" almost immediately after completing my training. My first clients were friends and neighbors who I practiced with. One of my neighbors wanted to lose weight. My "fee" to her was a spaghetti and meatball dinner every week that I worked with her. Another client was my roofer who wanted to stop smoking. My "fee" to him was cleaning my gutters. I would tell everyone who wanted to listen all about hypnosis. My first paying client was Doug, a young man who worked in the luncheonette where I bought my morning coffee. He wanted to lose weight. I had my office in a room in my house where I lived with my late husband and three-year-old son. I prearranged with my husband that when I had clients, they would go upstairs to the bedroom and watch TV.

Once, I had just induced hypnosis and was deepening the state when a little voice at the door piped up, "Mommy, I got to pee-pee." Hoping my client did not hear the "suggestion," I asked him to deepen his own hypnosis by slowly counting backward out loud from 100 down to 1 and that I would be back in a minute. I rushed out with Anton in tow, took him to the bathroom, and brought him back to my husband, who was sound asleep. I got back to my client, who was still counting 30, 29, 28 …

The first time I spoke about hypnosis, I was still in Dick Harte's internship program. A colleague of Dick's asked him if there was any student who would be willing to help him at a Learning

Annex class in self-hypnosis. He had laryngitis and couldn't speak loud enough for an extended period to be heard. He wanted someone to explain hypnosis, go over the formulation of suggestions with the class, and do the twenty-minute induction at the end of the class. He could still speak for short periods of time, but he needed someone to do these sections. Bruce would be there to assist me if needed. *What the heck*, I thought! I volunteered. The best way to learn to do something is to just jump in and do it.

Later, The Learning Annex invited me to teach self-hypnosis, weight management, and stop smoking at their newest locations in Brooklyn, NY, and Forest Hills, NY, in addition to their Manhattan HS locations. I was teaching three classes at three different locations three times a month. Can I keep it all straight? If it's Tuesday, it must be Brooklyn.

One time I showed up to do a weight management class in Brooklyn. I always arrived early. As the participants started to arrive, I noticed that not many of them seemed to need weight management. Then I saw that most of them went outside to have their last smoke before class. I had weight-loss material for a stop-smoking class. Since I had done weight-loss classes several times, I just winged it.

The first demonstration I did just months after I completed the internship was at a Lutheran conference at Silver Bay, Lake George, NY. I offered to do a short hypnosis demonstration. There were about twenty people there, including several pastors from various churches. One of the components of Richard's course was how to teach a three-week self-hypnosis course. Another component was how to do a hypnosis demo. I did a demonstration with one of the participants, who was the pastor of a Lutheran church. I suggested he couldn't bend his arm. His wife was sitting next to him. I suggested that he couldn't say his wife's name. He couldn't. We talked afterward, and he invited me to do a three-week self-hypnosis course at his church in White Plains, NY. The class went well. It was my first paid gig!

I took Richard Harte's "Train the Trainer" certified instructor course and then the advanced course in the mid-nineties. As I was teaching weight management, stop smoking, and self-hypnosis classes at a community college already, I proposed the 100-hour certification "Become a Certified Hypnotist" course to the college. I got the okay, and from September to December, we met every Monday and Wednesday night.

I continued to take training and buy books and DVDs. I attended conferences and offered to be a presenter. When I took my first training with Dick Harte, he told his class about the Association to Advance Ethical Hypnosis as he was the educational chair at that time. I was certified by the Association to Advance Ethical Hypnosis in 1987 and attended my first convention.

In the early nineties, I trained in stage hypnosis in Las Vegas with Jerry Valley, Tommy Vee, and Ormond McGill. I did some stage shows, locally with the most memorable one at the Fallsview Hotel, Ellenville, NY in the Catskills

In the mid-nineties, I partnered with Max Toth to form the International Center for Hypnosis. We did many training courses together. Eventually, we stopped teaching together, and I began to do my own training.

Around 1998, I got a call from another hypnotist who also lived in Yonkers and was looking for a fellow hypnotist to share an office. I jumped at it, and we shared a small office for many years.

I began teaching hypnosis classes at local colleges. I taught four two-hour courses offered in the fall and spring every year—self-hypnosis, weight management, stop smoking, and how to be a certified hypnotist. Many of the students who came to these classes became clients. During COVID-19, I continued to train as a hypnotist online with internationally known hypnotists.

I became board certified by the NGH in about 2010.

I have been a speaker at many hypnosis conventions since 1990.

In 2009, I began to teach the NGH-certified hypnosis course in my house. I was able to see clients and have students in an office on the second floor of my house. In the end of 2008, a gentleman, Robert Fried, who had been certified in 2005 in Hypnosis, NLP (Neurolinguistic Programming) and Timeline Therapy, called me because he wanted to learn more just about hypnosis. In 2006, Robert was one of many who attended my community college course on self-hypnosis and he tracked me down. So, in 2009 he became one of my students. One day, when Robert arrived for the class a little early, I introduced him to my husband, Tony. Robert asked me about my husband, who was disabled at the time. Robert, being a compassionate person, began coming early in the afternoon on the days we had class to spend time with my late husband, Tony. They became fast friends, and after the classes were over and Robert graduated as an NGH-certified hypnotist, the three of us became friends and began to "hang out" together. After my husband passed away in 2012, my good friend Robert was there to support me and help me through a difficult time. Our friendship blossomed into love, and in 2017, we were married.

I took training over the years from many different hypnotists; Dan Candell, Lisa Halpin, Roy Hunter, Jason Linett, Ormond McGill, Don Mottin, Richard Nongard, Jerry Valley, Tommy Vee, and others, too many to mention. To this day, I am still learning by attending conferences, taking online courses, and reading books.

In 2021, Robert and I became certified in NLP and Life Coaching.

My education is ongoing, and I continue to be awed and amazed by the power of hypnosis.

Currently, I see clients in person and online. You can visit my website www.joannabrahamsen.com and book a free Zoom consultation and appointments either in person or online.

Printed in Great Britain
by Amazon